Payroll—Manual and Computerised
Third Edition

Dympna Dolan

Gill & Macmillan

Gill & Macmillan Ltd
Hume Avenue
Park West
Dublin 12
with associated companies throughout the world
www.gillmacmillan.ie

© Dympna Dolan 2004
ISBN-13: 978 07171 3696 4

Print origination in Ireland by Carole Lynch

The paper used in this book is made from the wood pulp of managed forests. For every tree felled, at least one tree is planted, thereby renewing natural resources.

All rights reserved.
No part of this publication may be reproduced, copied or transmitted in any form or by any means without written permission of the publishers or else under the terms of any licence permitting limited copying issued by the Irish Copyright Licensing Agency.

A catalogue record is available for this book from the British Library.

Contents

NCVA Payroll Module Descriptor vi

PART 1 PAYROLL xi

Chapter 1
The PAYE system 1

Quiz
Explanation of Terms
Calculating Gross Pay
Questions on Gross Pay

Chapter 2
The Tax Credit System 8

The Tax Credit Certificate
Tax Credits in a Sample Tax Year
Tax Bands
The Standard Rate Cut-Off Point
Tax Credits in a Given Year
Calculating Tax Credits
Questions on Tax Credits

Chapter 3
Cumulative Tax System and PRSI 22

Quiz
Explanation of Terms
Pay Related Social Insurance (PRSI)
How to Calculate PRSI Contributions
Questions on PRSI Contributions
The Tax Credit System
The Cumulative Tax System
Questions on the Cumulative Tax System (First Set)
Questions on the Cumulative Tax System (Second Set)
Holiday Pay Calculation
Questions on the Cumulative Tax System (Third Set)
Questions on the Cumulative Tax System (Fourth Set)
Employees Starting Work During the Year
Change in Tax Credits During the Year
Questions on the Cumulative Tax System (Fifth Set)
Questions on the Cumulative Tax System (Sixth Set)

Chapter 4
Emergency and Temporary Tax Systems 49

Emergency Tax
Questions on Emergency Tax
Temporary Tax
Questions on Temporary Tax

Chapter 5
Tax Return Forms 60

Form P30 – Employer's Remittance Form
Form P45 – Cessation Certificate
Questions on Completing Form P45
Duties of an Employer at the End of the Tax Year
Form P60 – Certificate of Pay, Tax, and PRSI for an Employee
Questions on Completing Form P60
Forms P35L and P35 – Employer's Annual Return Forms
Question on Completing the Forms P35L and P35

PART 2 TAXATION 75

Chapter 6
Taxation – Treatment of Married Couples 77

Year of Marriage
Basis of Assessment for Married Couples
Single Assessment
Joint Assessment
Separate Assessment
Questions on the Single and Joint Assessment Methods

Chapter 7
Annual Take-Home Salary and Budgetary Changes 82

Calculating Take-Home Pay
Questions on Calculating Take-Home Pay
Effect of Budgetary Changes on Take-Home Pay
Questions on Calculating Take-Home Pay in Different Years

PART 3 COMPUTER PAYROLL 89

Chapter 8
Computer Payroll 91

Advantages of a Computerised Payroll System
Sample Exercise on a Computerised Payroll System
Sample Examination Papers

PART 4 REVISION 101

Chapter 9
Revision Assignments 103

Quiz
Revision Assignment 1
Revision Assignment 2
Sample FETAC Examination Material

Appendix A
Income Tax Calendar 118

Income Tax Weeks
Income Tax Months

Appendix B
PRSI Rates of Contribution for a Sample Tax Year 120

Class A PRSI Rates
Class B PRSI Rates
Class D PRSI Rates

Appendix C
PRSI Rates of Contribution for the Current Tax Year 123

Class A PRSI Rates
Class B PRSI Rates
Class D PRSI Rates

Appendix D
Tax Rates, Bands and Credits for the Current Tax Year 125

Tax Rates
Tax Bands
Tax Credits
Emergency Tax Data

Appendix E
Tax and PRSI Data for a Selection of Years 129

Appendix F
List of PAYE Forms That Employers Use 130

Appendix G
Copies of Various Tax Forms 132

List of Abbreviations 143

NCVA Payroll Module Descriptor

1	TITLE	PAYROLL – MANUAL AND COMPUTERISED
2	CODE	B20138
3	LEVEL	2
4	VALUE	1
5	PURPOSE	This module has been developed to provide the learner with the knowledge and skills to maintain payroll records manually and on computer in a small to medium-sized organisation.
6	PREFERRED ENTRY LEVEL	National Vocational Certificate, Leaving Certificate or equivalent qualifications and/or relevant life and work experience.
7	SPECIAL REQUIREMENTS	None.

8 **GENERAL AIMS**

This module aims to enable the learner to:

8.1 acquire the knowledge and skills necessary to use both manual and computerised payroll systems

8.2 understand the essential and appropriate terminology associated with personal taxation

8.3 appreciate the importance of accuracy and security in preparing and maintaining payroll records

8.4 acquire the knowledge and understanding of how the cumulative, emergency and temporary tax systems operate.

9 **UNITS**
Unit 1 **Manual Payroll**
Unit 2 **Computer Principles**
Unit 3 **Computer Payroll**

10 SPECIFIC LEARNING OUTCOMES

UNIT 1 MANUAL PAYROLL

The learner should be able to:

10.1.1 define the following terms: taxable income, gross pay, net pay, superannuation/pension, tax credits, standard rate cut-off point, gross tax, net tax, PAYE and PRSI

10.1.2 calculate gross pay for an employee to include basic pay, overtime, bonuses, commissions, holiday pay

10.1.3 calculate an employee's net annual tax credit for the year

10.1.4 explain the operation of the cumulative, emergency and temporary tax systems

10.1.5 complete cumulative tax deduction cards for employees

10.1.6 complete emergency and temporary tax deduction cards

10.1.7 calculate an employee's tax liability after moving from the emergency or temporary system to the cumulative system

10.1.8 calculate refunds to employees where appropriate

10.1.9 explain the purpose of the following statutory documents: P45, P60, P30, and P35

10.1.10 complete the following documents: P45, P60, P30, and P35

10.1.11 select the appropriate PRSI class for an employee

10.1.12 calculate an employee's liability for PRSI applying various PRSI classes

10.1.13 calculate an employer's liability for PRSI applying various PRSI classes

10.1.14 calculate the annual net pay of an employee to include: marital status, pension contributions, tax credits, and standard rate cut-off point

10.1.15 compare the tax liabilities for married couples who opt for separate or single assessment with those who opt for joint assessment

10.1.16 calculate the effects of the budget on an individual's take home pay.

UNIT 2 COMPUTER PRINCIPLES

The learner should be able to:

10.2.1 identify the main parts that make up a typical computer system in an accounts environment (e.g. CPU, monitor, keyboard, floppy disk, printer)

10.2.2 distinguish between hardware and software

10.2.3 distinguish between different operating systems (e.g. Windows and DOS)

10.2.4 perform the following file management functions: disk formatting, copying, backing up files in a directory/folder, creating a directory/folder, deleting files, copying a floppy disk

10.2.5 explain the advantages of computerised payroll over a manual payroll system

10.2.6 list a range of computerised payroll packages currently available

10.2.7 outline the importance of data accuracy when processing payroll data

10.2.8 explain the importance of data security and confidentiality in relation to computerised payroll

10.2.9 explain the importance of anti-virus protection software

10.2.10 identify the main features of the Data Protection Act.

UNIT 3 COMPUTER PAYROLL

The learner should be able to:

10.3.1 access a payroll package successfully

10.3.2 enter company details (e.g. name, address, registration number, bank sort code)

10.3.3 enter employee's details (e.g. name, address, marital status, PPS number, tax rates, tax credits, standard rate cut-off point, PRSI class and superannuation)

10.3.4 enter details regarding pay frequency (e.g. weekly, monthly) and method (e.g. cash, cheque, EFT)

10.3.5 enter details regarding payment types (e.g. overtime rates, bonus, commission, expenses, holidays, etc.)

10.3.6 enter details regarding non-statutory deductions for employees (e.g. pension, health insurance, trade union subscription)

10.3.7 process the payroll regularly for a number of employees

10.3.8 edit employee data where necessary (e.g. change in pay, change in tax credit, change in non-statutory deductions, etc.)

10.3.9 update records at end of period, i.e. close off transactions for week/month before starting next payroll run

10.3.10 print payroll management reports (e.g. total payroll cost per week/month, gross to net deduction list, employee cumulative payslips)

10.3.11 print relevant statutory document details (e.g. P45, P60, P30 and P35)

10.3.12 save data correctly according to appropriate system procedures

10.3.13 back up data according to appropriate system procedures

10.3.14 exit from software package properly

10.3.15 outline the importance of password protection.

11 PORTFOLIO ASSESSMENT

Project: The internal assessor will devise a project brief for candidates.

Examination: The internal assessor will devise a practical examination for candidates, to be held in a set period of time and under restricted conditions.

All assessment is externally moderated by the NCVA.

Summary: **Examination (Practical) 50%**
Project 50%

12 GRADING

Pass	50–64%
Merit	65–79%
Distinction	80–100%

Support Material for

PAYROLL—MANUAL AND COMPUTERISED 3RD EDITION

by Dympna Dolan

DYNAMIC AND EASY TO USE, ONLINE SUPPORT MATERIAL FOR THIS BOOK PROVIDES LECTURERS WITH:

- Taxation templates
- Tax return forms
- Blank payroll sheets

TO ACCESS LECTURER SUPPORT MATERIAL ON OUR SECURE SITE:

1) Go to www.gillmacmillan.ie/lecturers
2) Logon using your username and password. If you don't have a password, register online and we will email your password to you.

PROVIDES STUDENTS WITH:

- Taxation templates
- Tax return forms
- Blank payroll sheets

TO ACCESS STUDENTS SUPPORT MATERIAL:

1) Go to www.gillmacmillan.ie/student
2) Click on the link for Student Support material.

PART 1

Payroll

Chapter 1

The PAYE System

In this chapter you will learn:

- some of the essential terminology associated with the PAYE (Pay as You Earn) system
- how to calculate an employee's gross pay from given data.

The PAYE system came into operation in Ireland on 6 October 1960 for a limited number of employees, but it has been extended to cover almost everyone who is paid a wage or a salary. The PAYE system is the method used by the Revenue Commissioners to collect the following, based on an employee's income:

- income tax
- PRSI.

QUIZ

Before you read any further, have a look at the following true or false statements. Indicate your answer by circling the letter *T* or *F*.

1. **Gross pay:** this is an employee's pay only if he or she works forty hours per week. (T or F)
2. **Net pay:** this is an employee's take-home pay. (T or F)
3. **Basic pay:** this is the part of an employee's pay that is not taxed. (T or F)
4. **Wage:** this is money an employee receives if he or she works on a weekly basis only. (T or F)
5. **Salary:** this is money an employee (usually a manager) receives every month. (T or F)
6. **Superannuation:** this is a large (super) increase an employee receives in his or her annual (annuation) salary. (T or F)
7. **Statutory deduction:** this is a fixed deduction from an employee's pay (i.e. it's stationary). (T or F)
8. **Non-Statutory deduction:** this is a deduction from pay that can change from week to week. (T or F)
9. **Public sector employee:** a person who works in a large company dealing with the public. (T or F)
10. **Private sector employee:** a person who works in a family-owned business only. (T or F)

Now compare your answers with those on page 7. Then read the following explanations.

EXPLANATION OF TERMS

Gross Pay

This is an employee's pay of any kind, which may consist of up to thirty different components. The most common ones are: salary, wage, overtime, bonus, commission, holiday pay, Christmas box, tea money, back pay, workplace pensions, benefits-in-kind (e.g. company car), piece pay (e.g. strawberry pickers who are paid €1.00 per punnet picked) and disability benefit. Gross pay of any description is taxable.

Net Pay

Though commonly referred to as take-home pay, this is actually the amount of an employee's gross pay less:

- any ordinary pension contributions (i.e. approved by the Revenue Commissioners) made by the employee to the employer's scheme
- contributions to Revenue-approved permanent health benefit schemes, which are sometimes referred to as 'salary protection' or 'income continuance' plans.

The employer deducts these contributions from gross pay before calculating the amounts due for tax and PRSI.

Basic Pay

This is the pay an employee receives for working a regular thirty-nine or forty-hour week (if paid weekly). It is pay earned *without* any overtime payments, bonuses, etc. Other commonly used terms for this pay include: 'standard', 'ordinary' and 'flat' pay. Basic pay is taxable.

Wage

This is an amount of money (payment) earned by an employee for work done. It is usually calculated on an hourly basis. For example, Mary works a thirty-nine-hour week and she is paid €8.00 per hour. Her gross wage is €312.00 (i.e. 39 x €8.00). Another method of calculating a wage is by piece-rate pay. For example, a strawberry picker who fills 400 punnets and is paid €1.00 per punnet receives a wage of €400.00.

A wage may vary from week to week or month to month. This depends on the number of hours worked, overtime, bonuses, etc.

Salary

A salary is a fixed sum of money (payment) earned by an employee for work done. The payment (which may be paid on a weekly, fortnightly or monthly basis), unlike a wage, does not change. However, if an employee receives an increase in salary (e.g. with a promotion) then the fixed payment is adjusted on a weekly, fortnightly or monthly basis thereafter.

Superannuation

This commonly-used term means 'pension'. A pension is a deduction from an employee's gross pay. Certain employees in the public service have pension automatically deducted from their gross pay, whereas employees in the private sector are not obliged to join pension schemes. Normally pension contributions are calculated as a percentage of an employee's standard or basic pay. The government introduced new pension legislation effective from January 2003. The main initiative was the introduction of Personal Retirement Savings Accounts, known as PRSAs. Since September 2003 all employers are obliged to offer all their employees access to some form of pension arrangement. PRSAs are flexible pension plans. This means that an employee is entitled to stop, start or vary the contributions to their pensions as they choose. Furthermore, an employee on leaving service is entitled to take their PRSA with them and continue to contribute to the plan elsewhere.

An employee's contributions to PRSA automatically entitle him or her to the benefit of income tax relief. This means that the PRSA amount is deducted from gross pay before the calculation of income tax and PRSI.

Statutory Deduction

A statutory deduction is an amount of money taken from an employee's gross pay over which he or she has no control. The term statutory comes from the word 'state'. The following are statutory deductions:

- income tax
- PRSI
- superannuation contributions by some (public sector) employees.

Non-Statutory Deduction

A non-statutory deduction is an amount of money taken from an employee's net pay *after* tax and PRSI have been deducted. It is a voluntary deduction from pay agreed between the employee and the employer. Examples include union dues, health insurance (VHI or BUPA), company loan and social club.

Public Sector Employee

A public sector employee is one who is employed by the government or by a government agency. Teachers, nurses, the Garda Siochana, and RTE staff are all public sector employees.

Private Sector Employee

A private sector employee is one who works in any non-government employment. Accountants, mechanics, sales representatives, shop and factory workers are all private sector employees. They may be employed in a range of business or organisation types, from a small family-owned firm to a large multinational corporation.

Summary – Calculating Take-Home Pay

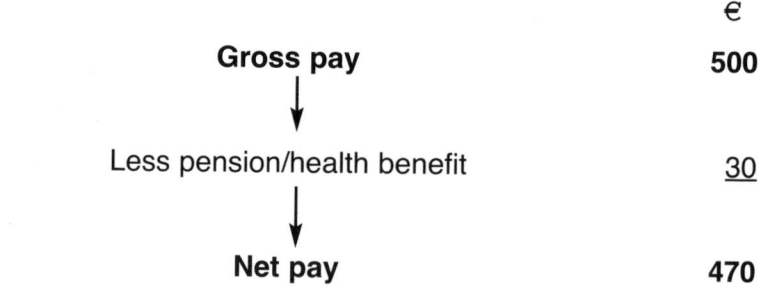

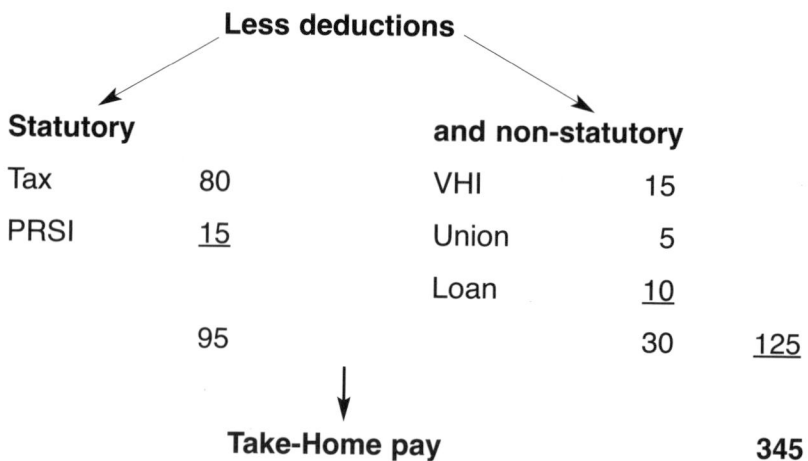

Figure 1.1 on page 5 shows a payslip or advice slip.

FIGURE 1.1 PAYSLIP OR ADVICE SLIP

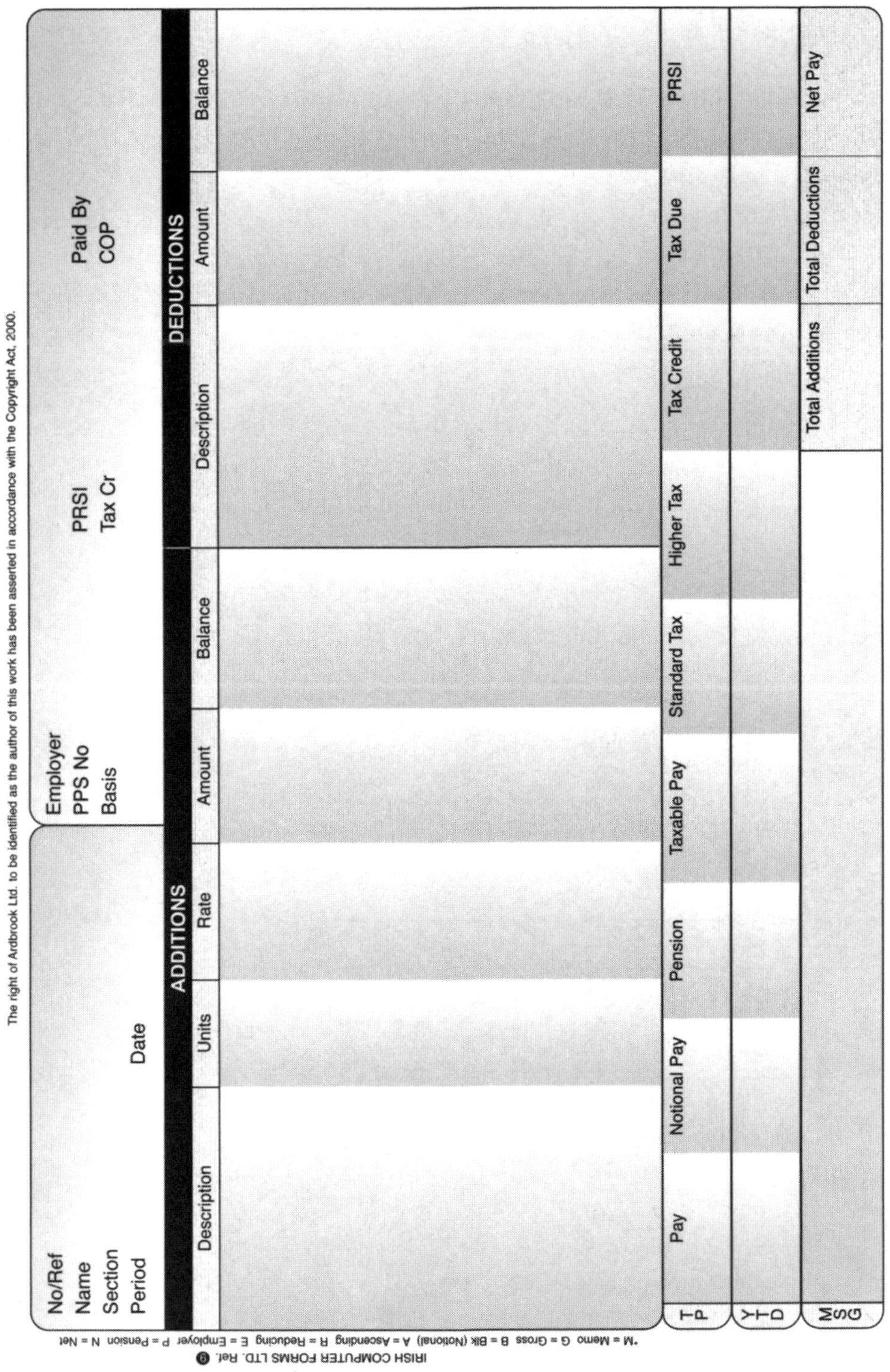

CALCULATING GROSS PAY

Gross pay includes a number of payment types such as wages, overtime, bonuses, etc.

Example 1.1

Margaret Dolan worked a thirty-nine-hour week (ordinary) for which she is paid €8.50 per hour. She also worked the following overtime hours during the week:

- Monday – two hours
- Tuesday – three hours
- Thursday – two hours
- Saturday – two hours.

Assume the overtime rates are as follows:

from Monday to Friday –

- the first hour is paid time plus one-quarter
- the second hour is paid time plus one-half
- the third and subsequent hours are paid double time.

On Saturday –

- the first two hours are paid time plus one-half
- the third and subsequent hours are paid double time.

The calculation of Margaret's gross pay is as follows.

Overtime

Day	x 1.25	x 1.50	x 2
Monday	1	1	0
Tuesday	1	1	1
Thursday	1	1	0
Saturday	0	2	0
Total	3.75	7.50	2.0

Total of overtime hours: 13.25
Ordinary hours: 39.00
Total hours worked: 52.25

The gross pay calculation is as follows:

52.25 hours x €8.50 per hour = €444.13

The PAYE System

QUESTIONS ON GROSS PAY

Calculate the gross pay for the following employees. Use the overtime rates given in Example 1.1 on the previous page.

1. Anne Ryan worked a forty-hour (ordinary) week and is paid €9.25 per hour. She also worked the following overtime hours during the week:
   - Monday – one hour
   - Tuesday – two hours
   - Saturday – four hours.
2. Jenny O'Halloran worked a normal thirty-nine-hour week and is paid €8.70 per hour. She also worked three hours of overtime on Wednesday and three hours on Saturday. She works as a sales representative and she is paid 2% commission on her sales (back week). Last week she sold €4,000 worth of goods.
3. Eileen McNeela worked a normal thirty-nine-hour week and she is paid €9.80 per hour. She works as a sales representative and she is paid 2% commission on her sales (back week) that are valued over €5,000. Last week her sales total came to €15,000.
4. Tom Jones worked a normal forty-hour week and he is paid €15.00 per hour. He is paid on a fortnightly basis. In his first week, he worked two hours of overtime on Monday and two hours on Thursday. He did not work any overtime in the second week, but received a performance bonus of €80.00 as part of his pay.
5. Tony Ambler worked a normal forty-hour week and he is paid €20.00 per hour. He is paid on a fortnightly basis. In his first week, he worked one hour of overtime on Monday and three hours on Saturday. In the second week, he worked two hours of overtime on Wednesday, and four hours on Saturday. He received a bonus of €75.00 as part of his pay.

Quiz Answers

All the statements are *false*.

Chapter 2

The Tax Credit System

In this chapter you will learn:

- some more terminology associated with the PAYE system
- the purpose of the Certificate of Tax Credits and Standard Rate Cut-Off Point
- the current rates of tax, tax bands and some of the main tax credits/reliefs.

> **Note:**
> Throughout this book *sample* tax and PRSI rates and other taxation details are used for explanation purposes. This is because these rates and other relevant details vary from year to year with the passing of each Finance Act.

Finding Current Information on Tax and PRSI Details

You can find the relevant, up-to-date information on tax and PRSI by contacting the following information offices and by accessing the web addresses mentioned:

- Your local tax office. The Revenue Commissioners have in place a regional structure to simplify and streamline the way in which they deliver services to their customers. As a PAYE employee, your tax affairs are now dealt with in the region *where you live.*
- Revenue Commissioners Customer Service, telephone Lo-call 1890 - 60 50 90
- Revenue Forms and Leaflets Service, telephone Lo-call 1890 - 30 67 06
- end-of-year forms at the Office of the Collector-General, P35 Section, Government Buildings, Nenagh, Co. Tipperary. Telephone Lo-call 1890 - 25 45 65
- The Revenue website is very good and can be accessed on **www.revenue.ie**; also the Revenue On-Line Service (ROS) at **www.ros.ie** is particularly useful for employers who want to file their returns electronically (e-filers) and who want to access information online
- PRSI queries can be made at your local Social Welfare Office or at the Department of Social and Family Affairs Gandon Hse, Amiens St, Dublin 1, telephone: (01) 7043274
- The Welfare website can be accessed on **www.welfare.ie**

> **Note:**
> The tax year starts on 1 January and ends on 31 December.

THE CERTIFICATE OF TAX CREDITS AND STANDARD RATE CUT-OFF POINT

If you are working at present or have worked in the past, you are probably familiar with a Certificate of Tax Credits and Standard Rate Cut-Off Point. This certificate is more commonly referred to as the 'tax credit certificate'. It is issued to taxpayers in December in time for the start of the tax year. You will be guided through the meaning and use of this certificate in this chapter.

It is the responsibility of *an employee* to ensure that he or she has an up-to-date tax credit certificate. An employee starting work for the first time must complete a form 12A (Income Tax Return form) giving details such as name, address, pay, etc. and send it to the Revenue Commissioners. The tax credit certificate is then issued and it is usually updated on an annual basis.

It is also the responsibility of the employee to complete an annual tax return form (form 11) if requested by the Revenue Commissioners. The two main purposes of this form are:

- to declare the total amount and sources of income (as accurately as possible)
- to claim tax credits.

A tax credit certificate contains the following essential information:

- employee's name, address, and PPS (Personal Public Service) number, formerly known as RSI (Revenue and Social Insurance) number
- employee's tax credits and standard rate cut-off point
- tax rates
- employer's registered number.

The Revenue Commissioners issue a summary (abbreviated) version of the employee's tax credit certificate to the employer. This tax credit certificate does not list the credits to which an employee is entitled, thereby safeguarding his or her privacy. If an employee has more than one job at the same time (e.g. full-time job during the day and part-time job in the evening) a separate tax credit certificate is issued to each employer. The tax office will allocate the appropriate tax credits and cut-off point to each employer based on the information supplied by the employee or on a request made by him or her.

Figure 2.1 on page 11 shows a sample tax credit certificate (employee part). Figure 2.2 on page 12 shows a sample tax credit certificate (employer part).

A tax credit certificate may be valid for one year or for more than one year (i.e. multi-year). An instruction printed on the top of the certificate will indicate that it is valid for one of the following:

- The year 20.. and following years commencing 1 January 20 ..
- For the year 20.. only commencing 1 January 20...

If the certificate is in the first category, the employer will continue to use it as the basis for tax deduction for each succeeding income tax year until the tax office issues an amended or adjusted certificate. In almost all cases, a tax credit certificate is valid for one year only, because of changes introduced in each Budget – more about this later on.

The tax office will amend a tax credit certificate if it discovers errors on the certificate. It will also amend a certificate at the request of an employee if the relevant information to make the amendment(s) is supplied to the tax office by the employee. When a tax credit certificate is amended a new one is issued to the employee. The employer will also be issued with the new version (abbreviated) if he or she is using the 'own system' for calculating tax. This is dealt with in more detail in Chapter 3.

It is the *employer's* responsibility to always operate PAYE on the basis of the certificate showing the *most recent* date of issue.

Note: Under no circumstances should an employer or employee make changes to a tax credit certificate.

The Tax Credit System

FIGURE 2.1 TAX CREDIT CERTIFICATE (EMPLOYEE PART)

INCOME TAX - PAY AS YOU EARN
NOTICE OF DETERMINATION OF TAX CREDITS AND STANDARD RATE CUT-OFF POINT
FOR THE YEAR 1ST JAN 2004 TO 31 DECEMBER 2004
AND FOLLOWING YEARS

When calling or writing to the Tax Office - always quote

Unit No.	Employer Number	PPS Number
001		

When calling or writing to the Department of Social and Family Affairs always quote your PPS Number.

TAX CREDITS				STANDARD RATE CUT-OFF POINT	
SINGLE TAX CREDIT			1520	STANDARD RATE BAND	28000
PAYE TAX CREDIT			1040		
TRADE UNION SUB CREDIT			40		
INCREASED BY	AMOUNT	@ 20%		INCREASED BY AMOUNT	
EXPENSES	1541	309		1541	
TOTAL INCREASES			309		1541
REDUCED BY				REDUCED BY AMOUNT	
OTHER SCHEDULE D INCOME	1210	242		1210	
TOTAL REDUCTIONS			242		1210

Net Tax Credits	2667	Standard Rate Cut-Off Point	28331	
Allocated to other employments	0	Allocated to other employments	0	
Tax Credits this employment €	2667	Cut-Off Point this employment €	28331	
Monthly Tax Credit €	222.25	Monthly Cut-Off Point €	2360.92	
Weekly Tax Credit €	51.29	Weekly Cut-Off Point €	544.83	
Standard Rate of Tax	20%	Higher Rate of Tax	42%	

The Tax Credits and Standard Rate Cut-Off Point have been advised to your employer

Issued By
INSPECTOR OF TAXES
FINGAL REVENUE DISTRICT
BLOCK D, ASHTOWN GATE
NAVAN ROAD
970 DUBLIN 15   PH 1890 33 34 25

Please see important notes overleaf.

Date of Issue   16 JAN 04   P2

12 Payroll—Manual and Computerised

FIGURE 2.2 TAX CREDIT CERTIFICATE (EMPLOYER PART)

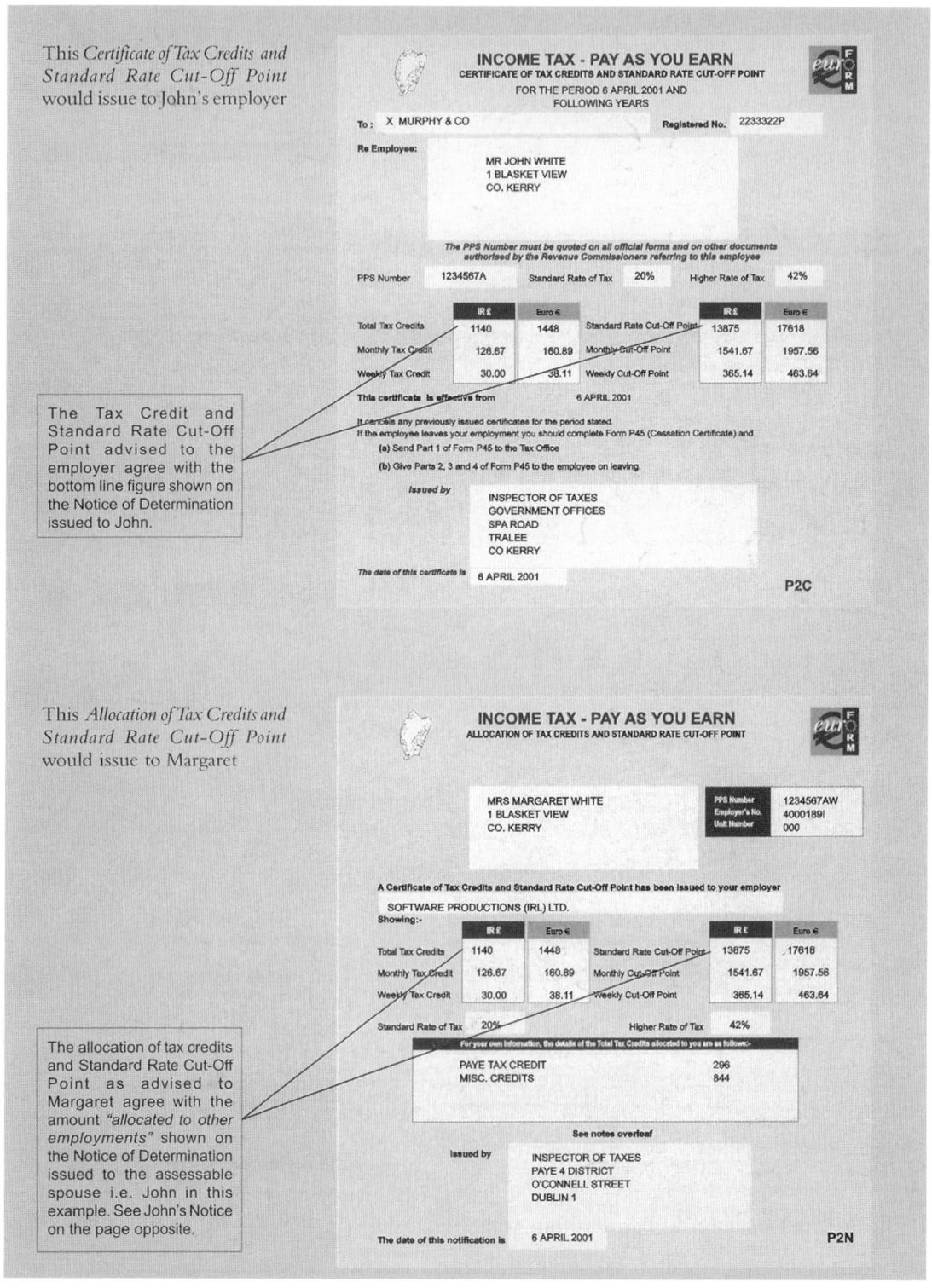

The Tax Credit System

TAX RATES

Table 2.1 shows information on the tax rates for a given year. You may insert the tax rates for the current tax year yourself in the column entitled 'Current Rate'.

TABLE 2.1 TAX RATES

Description	Rate	Current Rate
Standard Rate	20 %	
Higher Rate	42 %	

The amount of the employee's tax credit is adjusted to take account of any non-PAYE income or 'coded income'. Examples include rental income, investment income and social welfare pensions. Such coded income due at the higher rate of tax will have the effect of reducing the tax credit. The reduction in the credit will be the amount of the income allowed at the standard rate of tax. On the other hand, employment expenses to which an employee is entitled will increase the tax credit. See Figure 2.1 on page 11.

TAX BANDS

A tax band is a fixed amount of taxable income that is taxed at the standard rate of tax. Any taxable pay exceeding the band amount is taxed at the higher rate.

Table 2.2 shows information on the tax bands and tax rates for a given year. You may insert the information for the current tax year yourself in the column entitled 'Bands of Taxable Income in the Current Tax Year'.

TABLE 2.2 TAX BANDS

Personal Status	Bands of Taxable Income in a Sample Tax Year	Bands of Taxable Income in the Current Tax Year
Single / widowed without dependent child(ren)	€28,000 @ 20% Balance @ 42%	€ @ % Balance @ %
Single / widowed with dependent child(ren)*	€32,000 @ 20% Balance @ 42%	€ @ % Balance @ %
Married couple (one spouse with income)	€37,000 @ 20% Balance @ 42%	€ @ % Balance @ %
Married couple (both spouses with income)	€37,000 @ 20% (with an increase of €19,000 max) Balance @ 42%	€ @ % (with an increase of € max) Balance @ %

* A dependent child is one who satisfies one of the following criteria:
- under sixteen years of age
- over sixteen years of age and in receipt of full-time education or training since the beginning of the tax year.

Tax bands have been 'individualised' for married couples since 2000. The following example illustrates this point. The information in Table 2.2 above for a sample tax year is used in the calculations.

Example 2.1
Mike and Teresa Horan, a married couple, earn €36,000 and €40,000 respectively. Their income, as single individuals, is taxed as follows:

Mike
€28,000 @ 20% = €5,600
€ 8,000 @ 42% = €3,360
€36,000 Tax   = €8,960

Teresa
€28,000 @ 20% = € 5,600
€12,000 @ 42% = € 5,040
€40,000 Tax   = €10,640

Total Tax = €19,600

As a couple the calculation is as follows:

Band   €56,000 @ 20% = €11,200 (€37,000 + €19,000)
Balance   €20,000 @ 42% = € 8,400
          €76,000   €19,600

The calculation of tax due by married couples is dealt with in more detail in Chapter 6.

QUESTIONS ON TAX BANDS
Calculate the income tax due by Tom and Helen, a married couple. Calculations are to be based on married couple status and as single individuals. Use Example 2.1 as a guide.

1. Tom earns €42,000 and Helen earns €31,000.

2. Tom earns €29,500 and Helen earns €45,000.

3. Tom earns €50,000 and Helen earns €36,000.

THE STANDARD RATE CUT-OFF POINT

The standard rate cut-off point is the amount of income up to which point tax is charged at the standard rate. Any income earned above this point is taxed at the higher rate. The cut-off point amount is the same as the tax band but it is adjusted for any non-PAYE income (coded income). Typically, investment or rental income is non-PAYE income. Therefore, the cut-off point will be adjusted to take this into account.

The standard rate cut-off point varies from person to person, depending on personal circumstances. The total tax credit is also adjusted at the standard rate of tax to allow for any non-PAYE income (see Figure 2.1). The following examples show how the standard rate cut-off point may vary from one person to another. The information in Table 2.2 is used to explain.

Example 2.2

Sonya Curley is a single person earning €32,000. She is taxed as follows:

Band (Cut-off Point)	€28,000 @ 20%	=	€5,600
Balance	€ 4,000 @ 42%	=	€1,680
	€32,000		€7,280

Example 2.3

Sean and Kathrina Mooney, a married couple, earn €38,000 and €40,000 respectively. Sean has shares in a company and his investment income is €2,000. The couple is taxed in the following way:

Band (Cut-off Point)	€56,000		
Non-PAYE income	€ 2,000		
	€54,000 @ 20%	=	€10,800
Balance	€24,000 @ 42%	=	€10,080
	€78,000 Tax	=	€20,880

or, as individuals, it is:

Sean				Kathrina			
*€26,000 @ 20%	=	€5,200		€28,000 @ 20%	=	€5,600	
€12,000 @ 42%	=	€5,040		€12,000 @ 42%	=	€5,040	
€38,000				€40,000			
Tax	=	€10,240		Tax		=	€10,640

Total Tax = €20,880

*This is (€28,000 – €2,000 non-PAYE income)

Note: The tax *credit* for this couple is also reduced by the non-PAYE income. The amount is €400 and is calculated as follows: €2,000 @ 20%. All adjustments required to arrive at the standard rate cut-off point and tax credits for individual employees will be made by the tax office.

The tax office calculates the standard rate cut-off point for each taxpayer and this figure appears on the taxpayer's tax credit certificate, see Figure 2.1. If employers are using the official manual of tax deduction cards for their employees, the tax office types the cut-off point amount in the appropriate column on the card for every week of the year - more about this in Chapter 3.

QUESTIONS ON STANDARD RATE CUT-OFF POINT

Calculate the income tax due by Kevin and Adrienne, who are taxed as a married couple and as single individuals. Use Example 2.3 as a guide.

1. Kevin earns €44,000 and Adrienne earns €34,000. Adrienne also earns investment income worth €3,200

2. Kevin earns €36,000 and Adrienne earns €30,000. Kevin also earns rental income worth €4,000

TAX CREDITS

Employees can claim a number of credits or allowances which help reduce their tax bill.

Table 2.3 lists the main tax credits for a given tax year. You may insert the figures for the current year in the column entitled 'Tax Credits Current Year'.

Incapacitated Child Credit

This credit is subject to the following conditions:

- the child must be under *sixteen* years of age and be permanently incapacitated due to intellectual or physical disability
- the child is over *sixteen* years of age (on 1 Jan. of the tax year), is permanently incapacitated, and had become so before the child reached twenty-one years of age
- the child is over *twenty-one* years of age and has become permanently incapacitated, but had been in receipt of full-time education or full-time training with an employer for a period of not less than two years.

The credit is also available for incapacitated adopted children, stepchildren and children of unmarried parents.

The Tax Credit System

TABLE 2.3 TAX CREDITS

Personal Status	Tax Credits Sample Year €	Tax Credits Current Year €
Single Person	1,520	
Married Person	3,040	

Widowed Person
    Without dependent child(ren)
    With dependent child(ren)
	
	1,820
	1,520	

One-Parent Family
    Widowed Person
    Other Person
	
	1,520
	1,520	

Widowed Parent
    Bereaved in   Year 1
                      Year 2
                      Year 3
                      Year 4
                      Year 5
	
	2,600
	2,100
	1,600
	1,100
	600	

PAYE (individual)	1,040	
Incapacitated Child (max)	500	
Dependent Relative (max)	60	
Home Carer (max)	770	
Trade Union Subscription (max)	40	

Dependent Relative Credit

The following conditions must be satisfied to claim this credit:

- the dependent relative must be related to the taxpayer or to the taxpayer's spouse
- the taxpayer must prove that the relative is maintained at his or her expense
- the dependent relative must be incapacitated (e.g. old age, illness) and be unable to maintain himself or herself unless the dependant is the taxpayer's widowed mother or the widowed mother of the taxpayer's spouse
- the dependent relative's income must not exceed the qualifying limit which is established before the start of the tax year. If the relative's income exceeds this limit no tax credit is due.

The Home Carer's Credit

A married couple may claim this credit where one spouse (the home carer) cares for one or more dependent persons. Only one credit is due irrespective of the number of persons being cared for. The credit is not available to married couples who are taxed as single persons. Neither is it allowed to dual-income married couples with combined incomes in excess of the married couple tax band.

Under What Conditions is the Home Carer's Credit Granted?

To receive the home carer's credit the following conditions must be met:

- the home carer must care for one or more dependent persons, a dependent person being
  - a child for whom Child Benefit is payable
  - a person aged sixty-five years or over
  - a person who is permanently incapacitated due to physical or mental infirmity
- the dependent person(s) must normally reside with the married couple for the tax year.

OTHER ALLOWABLE CREDITS (RELIEFS)

Medical Expenses Relief

A taxpayer may claim relief on medical expenses which were incurred during the tax year and which were not reimbursed by a health insurer (i.e. VHI or BUPA) or local Health Authority. Allowable expenses include doctor and hospital visits, physiotherapy and prescribed medicines and drugs. Routine dental treatment is not allowable.

To claim relief, the taxpayer must submit a Form MED.1 to the tax office, detailing the qualifying expenses incurred. The taxpayer must retain receipts for all qualifying expenditure for inspection by the Inspector of Taxes. The relief for any tax year is based on the actual medical expenditure incurred during that year. When calculating the amount of relief due, both individuals and families are disallowed from claiming a certain fixed amount. The remainder of the relief above this amount is fully allowable.

Medical Insurance

Tax relief may be claimed on the insurance premium paid to a Revenue-approved health insurer (e.g. VHI, BUPA) for medical cover. The tax relief is given at source (TRS). Relief is allowed at the standard rate of tax and then netted off against the premium paid by the taxpayer. The medical insurer claims the amount given as tax relief from the government. For example: Claire pays €500.00 medical insurance premium to the VHI. The net cost of her insurance is calculated as follows:

Insurance premium	=	€500.00
Tax relief	=	€100.00 (i.e. €500 x 20%)
Net premium cost	=	€400.00

The VHI claims the tax relief of €100.00, granted to Claire from the government.

Mortgage Interest Relief

A mortgage loan is defined as a loan used by an individual solely for the purpose of the purchase, repair, development or improvement of a private residence (home). This residence must be the main or only one of the taxpayer.

The relief is available on the mortgage *interest* that is paid in any tax year and not on the mortgage repayment itself. For example, an individual pays €25,000 to a building society during the year of which €14,000 is interest. Only the €14,000 is allowable for tax relief.

In granting relief, the tax office makes a distinction between the first-time buyers of a home and all other mortgage holders. The maximum amount of interest allowable for tax relief purposes for first-time buyers is slightly higher than that for other mortgage holders (see Table 2.4). The period for this preferential treatment lasts for *seven* years. This is determined by the tax year in which the *first* claim for mortgage interest relief was made by the taxpayer. For example, if a taxpayer first claimed interest relief in 2004, then he or she qualifies for the first-time-buyers' relief for the last time in 2010 (i.e. seven years from 2004). From then on the taxpayer is entitled to the non-first-time-buyers' relief.

Since 1 Jan. 2002 mortgage interest relief, at the standard rate of tax, is granted at source (TRS), similarly to the medical insurance relief. This means that the tax relief on the mortgage interest is 'built into' the monthly mortgage repayment, which is made to the building society or bank. The mortgage repayment will be reduced by the amount of the tax credit.

Table 2.4 shows information on mortgage interest relief.

TABLE 2.4 MORTGAGE INTEREST RELIEF IN A SAMPLE YEAR

Marital Status	First-Time Buyer Maximum Interest	First-Time Buyer Maximum Tax Credit	Non-First-Time Buyer Maximum Interest	Non-First-Time Buyer Maximum Tax Credit
	€	€	€	€
Single	4,000	800	2,540	508
Widowed/Married	8,000	1,600	5,080	1,016

For example, Kaye McDonnell, a single person, paid €5,500 mortgage interest. She claimed interest for the first time last year, therefore she qualifies for first-time-buyer's relief. The net amount of her interest is calculated as follows:

Mortgage interest = €5,500
Tax relief (credit) = €   800 (i.e.€4,000 x 20%)
Net interest = €4,700

Finally, if the mortgage interest paid by an individual in the tax year is *below* the maximum relief (credit) allowable, then relief is claimed on *this* amount.

There are many more credits and reliefs which an individual can claim, such as age and blind person's credits, service charges, rent relief, covenants and fees paid to approved colleges.

However, as these are not required for examination in the FETAC Payroll-Manual and Computerised module (Level 2) they are not dealt with in this book.

CALCULATING TAX CREDITS

The following examples show how to calculate tax credits in a sample tax year. Calculations are based on the information in Table 2.3 for a sample tax year.

Example 2.4

David McEntee is a single person. He pays €150.00 trade union subscription.

Solution

	€
Single credit	1,520
PAYE credit	1,040
Trade union sub.	30
Total tax credit	2,590

Example 2.5

Anne Ryan is a widow for the last two years. She has two children aged six and nine. She also paid €125 house insurance.

Solution

	€
Widow credit	1,520
One-parent family	1,520
Widowed parent all.	2,100
PAYE credit	1,040
Total tax credit	6,180

Note: House insurance is not allowable as a tax credit.

Example 2.6

Brian and Anne Moloney are a married couple. They have a seven-year-old daughter with special needs and Brian's aged mother lives with the family. Their combined credits are:

Notes: The monthly tax credit is €215.83 (€2,590 ÷ 12).
The weekly tax credit is €49.81 (€2,590 ÷ 52).
The trade union subscription is allowed at the standard rate of tax. The maximum allowable is €200.

Solution

	€
Married credit	3,040
PAYE credit	2,080
Incapacitated child	500
Dependent relative	60
Total tax credit	5,680

QUESTIONS ON TAX CREDITS

Calculate the annual tax credit for the current tax year for the following employees. Use the relevant information for the *current* tax year in your calculations (see Appendix D, or Table 2.3 on page 16).

If you want you can also calculate the following for each employee:

- the monthly tax credit, by dividing the annual total by twelve
- the weekly tax credit, by dividing the annual total by fifty-two. Do not divide the monthly figure by four. Think about it.

1. Marion King is a single person. She pays €185.00 trade union subscription.
2. Paul McGrail is a single person. He pays €300.00 trade union subscription.
3. Thomas Reilly is a widower for three years.
4. Rita Carroll is a widow for two years. She pays €85.00 trade union subscription.
5. Helen Shaw is a widow for eight years. She has two children aged ten and twelve.

Calculate the combined tax credits for the following married couples:

6. Kevin and Betty Clancy, with no dependent children.
7. Derek and Teresa Timmons. Derek's elderly mother lives with the family and is maintained by them.
8. Robert and Mary Kiely. They have a seven-year-old child with special needs.
9. Tom and Anne Smith. They have a nineteen-year-old son with special needs who is attending college.

Chapter 3

Cumulative Tax System and PRSI

In this chapter you will learn:

- the terminology associated with the cumulative tax system and PRSI
- how to operate the cumulative tax system and complete tax deduction cards (TDCs) on a weekly and monthly basis
- how to deal with holiday (annual leave) payments
- how to deal with an employee who starts work during the tax year
- how to deal with a change in a taxpayer's tax credits during the tax year.

QUIZ

It's quiz time again! Have a go at the following true or false statements. To indicate your answer, circle the letter *T* or *F*.

1. A registered employer is one who is entitled to vote. (T or F)
2. PPS means Personal Pension Scheme. (T or F)
3. 'Cumulative' means adding together present and previous totals. (T or F)
4. A tax deduction card is one that is taken (deducted) from you when you leave work. (T or F)
5. 'Holiday pay' is not taxed. (T or F)
6. If a permanent employee is absent from work due to illness, the employee does not get paid. (T or F)
7. All employers receive payment from the Revenue Commissioners for collecting tax and PRSI on their behalf. (T or F)
8. The income tax calendar year starts on 1 January. (T or F)
9. The Revenue Commissioners accept computer payroll records from employers. (T or F)
10. PRSI means 'Pay your Relations Social Insurance'. (T or F)

Now check your answers on page 24. Read through the correct explanations.

EXPLANATION OF TERMS

1. A registered employer is one who has notified the Revenue Commissioners of his or her name and address and that he or she is paying an employee at least €8 per week (or €34 a month). An employer who is registered for PAYE is advised

formally of his or her registered number. An employer may have more than one registration number due to the following circumstances:
- an employer who has more than one branch may find it convenient to have each branch separately registered for PAYE/PRSI purposes
- an employer who keeps separate wage records for different groups of employees (e.g. office, factory, etc.) may wish to make separate PAYE/PRSI returns (remittances) under a separate registration number for each group
- separate registration is necessary where an employer has both permanent and casual employees, as casual employees are paid daily or at intervals of less than a week (by the way, if the registered employer is an individual over eighteen years of age, he or she is entitled to vote!).

2. PPS means Personal Public Service and it refers to a person's official identification number when dealing with any government department. An example is 3465889J. The PPS number was formerly called the RSI number (Revenue and Social Insurance) and it came into effect in April 2001. Holders of RSI numbers will keep their existing number but it will be referred to as the PPS number in future.

3. The cumulative tax system means that an employee's pay and tax credits are accumulated over the tax year. For example, if pay in week one is €300 and pay in week two is €400, then the cumulative pay at the end of week two is €700.

4. A tax deduction card (Form P9/P11) is one which is supplied by the tax office to the employer and on which the employer can record an employee's tax and PRSI deductions. A separate card is supplied for each employee of the firm or business.

5. Holiday pay is taxed – unfortunately!

6. If an employee is absent from work owing to illness, he or she may receive, or is entitled to receive, disability benefit or occupational injury benefit. These amounts are taxable in the hands of the employee, because they are regarded as 'income' or 'pay'.

7. If you are working at present, ask your employer this question. Just wait for the reply! The duties of all employers are as follow:
- to register with the Revenue Commissioners
- to keep PAYE/PRSI records on official forms or on an alternative approved record system
- to deduct tax (if any) and the employee's share of PRSI (if any) and keep records of the amounts
- to give a form P45 to an employee who ceases employment and advise the Inspector of Taxes of this occurrence
- to advise the Inspector of Taxes when an employee takes up or resumes employment
- to pay all the tax and PRSI contributions deducted during the month, to the Collector-General

- to complete end-of-year tax returns for the Revenue Commissioners
- to give each employee who is working with the employer a form P60 at the end of the tax year.

So that's the employer's lot.

8. The income tax calendar year starts on 1 January and ends on 31 December, effective from 1 January 2002. Previous to this, the tax year started on 6 April and ended on 5 April the following year. The 5 April year-end dates back to 1752 when the British government replaced its Roman calendar with the more accurate one introduced by Pope Gregory X111 in 1582. Ireland has operated the 5 April year-end from the foundation of the State in 1922 until now. The current 31 December year-end is in line with the practice in most European countries. There is an income tax calendar in Appendix A.

9. Yes, this is correct. An employer is *not* obliged to use the official tax deduction card (TDC) supplied by the tax office. Instead of using the this card, an employer may use one of the following:
   - a PAYE/PRSI record system of his or her own design
   - a commercially marketed manual system
   - a computerised system
   - the services of a computer bureau or agency.

   An employer who wants to use any of the alternative methods must first advise the Revenue Commissioners before using such a system. They can be contacted at the following address: P35 Section, Government Buildings, Nenagh, Co. Tipperary. All relevant information must be supplied. This office supplies end-of-year forms on continuous stationery suitable for computer processing. Alternatively, employers may use the ROS (Revenue-On-Line) service for making returns. Regardless of the system that employers choose, they must comply with the PAYE system of tax and PRSI collection.

10. Almost right! PRSI means Pay Related Social Insurance.

Quiz Answers:
1.False. 2.False. 3.True. 4.False. 5.False. 6.False. 7.False. 8.True. 9.True. 10.False.

PAY RELATED SOCIAL INSURANCE

Before starting the cumulative tax system let's do some work on PRSI. PRSI and a health contribution levy are charged on the gross pay (less superannuation and permanent health insurance) of a taxpayer under the PAYE system.

All income, with the exception of certain social welfare benefits, is liable for PRSI and the health contribution (from now on referred to as PRSI only). Since January 2004 all benefits-in-kind income is subject to PRSI contributions. Typically, a company car is treated as a benefit-in-kind. Most employees are liable to pay PRSI. The exceptions include individuals aged seventy or over, who are exempt from PRSI but not the health contribution. All employers are also obliged to pay their contribution to PRSI, based on their employee's pay.

There are nine different categories or 'classes' of PRSI. Most of them are divided into subclasses. For example, class A PRSI is divided as follows: A0, AX, A1, A2, A4, A5, A6, A7, A8 and A9. The majority of employees working in the private sector pay class A PRSI.

A fixed amount of an employee's gross pay (less superannuation and permanent health benefit) is PRSI-free under a number of the PRSI classes (i.e. the pay is not liable for PRSI), but it *is* liable for the health contribution levy. The employee pays a PRSI contribution on earnings above these fixed amounts. See Appendix C for the current amounts. The PRSI-free amount per week or per month is non-cumulative. This means that if it is not used in any week or month, then the benefit is lost. For example, if an employee (who is paid weekly) did not work in a particular week, then he or she cannot carry over the PRSI-free amount to the next week. The PRSI-free allowance does not apply to the employer's contribution towards PRSI.

Finally, the class of PRSI in which an employee is placed depends on a number of factors, some of which include the following:

- whether the employment is in the public or private sector; for example, permanent and pensionable employees recruited before 6 April 1995 in the public sector pay class D PRSI
- the nature of the employment; for example, self-employed people pay class S PRSI
- the earnings of the employee; for example, an employee earning less than €38 per week normally pays class J PRSI. Furthermore, an employee may be moved from one subclass of PRSI to another if his or her pay changes. For example, an employee on class A PRSI may pay class AX one week and class A1 in the next week. This situation could arise if the employee's pay in the second week is sufficiently large (perhaps because of overtime earnings) to cause him or her to be moved into a higher class for that particular week. This is illustrated in Example 3.4 on page 27.

> An up-to-date PAYE/PRSI information pack may be obtained from the Department of Social and Family Affairs, telephone 01-7043274.

HOW TO CALCULATE PRSI CONTRIBUTIONS

For information on the PRSI classes A, B and D in a given tax year, see Appendix B.

Example 3.1

Catherine Bruen earns €320.00 per week and she pays class AX PRSI.

Solution

(EE) Employee's share   €
    €127.00 x 0.00%   =   0.00
    €193.00 x 4.00%   =   7.72
    €320.00   7.72

(ER) Employer's share
    €320.00 x 8.50%   =   27.20

(Tot) Total contribution   =   34.92

Example 3.2

Darren McCallig earns €380.00 per week and he pays class A1 PRSI.

Solution

(EE) Employee's share   €
    €127.00 x 2.00%   =   2.54
    €253.00 x 6.00%   =   15.18
    €380.00   17.72

(ER) Employer's share
    €380.00 x 10.75%   =   40.85

(Tot) Total contribution   =   58.57

Example 3.3

Liz McCann earns €315.00 per week and she pays class BX PRSI.

Solution

(EE) Employee's share   €
    € 26.00 x 0.00%   =   0.00
    €289.00 x 0.90%   =   2.60
    €315.00   2.60

(ER) Employer's share
    €315.00 x 2.01%   =   6.33

(Tot) Total contribution   8.93

Example 3.4

Michael Edwards earns €330.00 per week and pays class AX PRSI. He works overtime on occasion and in his second week of work his total gross pay was €410.00.

Solution

Week No. 1 (class AX)
(EE) Employee's share   €
    €127.00 x 0.00%   =   0.00
    €203.00 x 4.00%   =   8.12
    €330.00   8.12

(ER) Employer's share
    €330.00 x 8.50%   =   28.05

(Tot) Total contribution   =   36.17

Week No. 2 (class A1)
(EE) Employee's share   €
    €127.00 x 2.00%   =   2.54
    €283.00 x 6.00%   =   16.98
    €410.00   19.52

(ER) Employer's share
    €410.00 x 10.75%   =   44.08

(Tot) Total contribution   =   63.60

Michael moved from class AX PRSI in week number one to class A1 in week number two. This is because his pay in week number two *exceeded* the income limit (threshold) for class AX PRSI. Therefore, all of his income is liable for class A1 PRSI for that week. If in week number three his pay goes back to €330.00, he will then be taxed at class AX PRSI again.

QUESTIONS ON PRSI CONTRIBUTIONS

Use the *current* rates of PRSI in your calculations (see Appendix C).

In each of the following cases, do the following:
- determine which class of PRSI the employee comes under from the details given
- calculate the total amount of PRSI (employer and employee), using the appropriate PRSI rates.

Note: PRSI is calculated on an employee's gross pay less contributions to the following:

(i) superannuation
(ii) permanent health benefit.

1. Gerard Silke works as a staff officer in his local bank earning €460.00 per week.
2. Angela O'Donoghue has been working in An Post since May 1997 earning €380.00 per week.
3. Robert Fitzgerald works as a dentist in the Dental Hospital earning €780.00 per week.
4. Kaite Cunningham has been working as a clerical officer in the Department of Finance since May 1990 earning €570.00 per week.
5. Roy Starr works as a senior buyer in Arnotts department store earning €650.00 per week.

THE TAX CREDIT SYSTEM

The tax credit system is fully operational in Ireland since 6 April 2001. It represents the largest overhaul of the taxation system since the introduction of PAYE in 1960.

Under this system, tax is calculated at the appropriate tax rates on an employee's gross pay (less pension and health benefit) in order to arrive at the gross tax. This gross tax is then reduced by the employee's tax credit, so as to arrive at the net tax payable.

The tax office will, in respect of *each employee*, notify the employer in December of the:

- tax credits
- standard rate cut-off point
- rates of tax.

> The 'standard rate cut-off point' will be referred to simply as the 'cut-off point' from now on (where most appropriate).

Example 3.5

Tax calculation under the tax credit system.

Anne Sweeney earns €600.00 per week. Her cut-off point is €540.00 per week and her tax credit is €45.00 per week. The tax calculation for the first week of the tax year for Anne is as follows:

Gross Pay	€600.00	
Tax on €540.00 @ 20%	€108.00	i.e. standard rate tax on the pay up to a maximum of the cut-off point
Tax on € 60.00 @ 42%	€ 25.20	i.e. higher rate tax on pay in excess of the cut-off point
Total gross tax	€133.20	
Less tax credit	€ 45.00	advised by the tax office
Total net tax this week	€ 88.20	

THE CUMULATIVE TAX SYSTEM

It is the duty of the employer at the start of the tax year to have either a tax deduction card (TDC) or a tax credit certificate for every employee for the coming tax year. If the employer has neither of them, then the 'emergency' or 'temporary' tax systems operate. These systems are dealt with in Chapter 4.

> **Note:**
> An employer is legally obliged to deduct tax and pay it to the Collector-General whether or not a tax credit certificate or TDC has been received.

An employer can use an official TDC or an approved alternative one for keeping payroll records of employees. Figure 3.1 shows an official TDC. Figure 3.2 shows an approved 'own system' TDC. Take a few minutes to examine them. Which one do you think is better and why?

FIGURE 3.1 OFFICIAL CUMULATIVE TAX DEDUCTION CARD

Revenue

TAX DEDUCTION CARD

TDCGA.FRM

Incorporating Certificate of Tax Credits and Standard Rate Cut-off Point

The Tax Credits and Standard Rate Cut-off Point set out on this card refer to

These instructions cancel any previously issued card for the year *to*

If you have any problems with the operation of this card please refer to the Notice to Employers issued by the Tax Office. You can obtain a copy by phoning your local Tax Office or in Dublin by phoning Revenue Forms and Leaflets Service at :
Lo-Call No. 1890 306 706.

EMPLOYER'S Name & Address

Employer's Number Date of Issue

This Tax Deduction Card is effective from

and should be implemented accordingly

EMPLOYEE DETAILS

PPS Number Works Number (N6)

Name Year TO

Total Tax Credit Total Cut-Off Point

Standard Tax Rate:	%
Higher Tax Rate:	%

Columns headed "For Employer's Use" may be used by YOU for making whatever entries YOU require e.g. net pay, employer's PRSI etc.

The PPS number must be quoted on all official forms and in any correspondence referring to this employee.

Issued by:

A Date of Payment	B See PAYE Calendar: Month	B See PAYE Calendar: Week	C PRSI Employee's Share €	C c	D PRSI Total Contribution €	D c	E Social Ins weekly record: Insurable Employment	E PRSI Class	F For Employer use (Net pay, Employers PRSI etc) €	F c
		1								
	1 Jan. to 31 Jan.	2								
		3								
		4								
	1	5								
		6								
	1 Feb. to 28 Feb.	7								
		8								
	2	9								
		10								
	1 Mar. to 31 Mar.	11								
		12								
	3	13								
		14								
	1 Apr. to 30 Apr.	15								
		16								
		17								
	4	18								
		19								
	1 May to 31 May	20								
		21								
	5	22								
		23								
	1 June to 30 June	24								
		25								
	6	26								
		27								
	1 July to 31 July	28								
		29								
		30								
	7	31								
		32								
	1 Aug. to 31 Aug.	33								
		34								
	8	35								
		36								
	1 Sept. to 30 Sept.	37								
		38								
	9	39								
		40								
	1 Oct. to 31 Oct.	41								
		42								
		43								
	10	44								
		45								
	1 Nov. to 30 Nov.	46								
		47								
	11	48								
		49								
	1 Dec. to 31 Dec.	50								
		51								
		52								
	12	53								
		K3					Total Weeks			
		K4					F2			

P9/P11	If the person to whom this card refers is not now in your employment or leaves your employment before 31st December next please return this card to the address shown above. If employee leaves your employment during the year to which this card refers, you should complete form P45 Cessation Certificate	C2 Initial Class	**Social Insurance Class** IF Class changed during this employment complete these boxes: Date of Change B4; Other Class C3; Weeks at Other Class F3

N.B If more than two classes please furnish details on Form PRC 1

Cumulative Tax System and PRSI

TDCGE.FRM

Employee's Name	PPS Number	Works No.	Total Tax Credit	Total Cut-Off	Date of Issue

Week No.	G Gross Pay (less Superannuation) this Period	H Cumulative Gross Pay to Date	I Cumulative Standard Rate Cut-Off point	J Cumulative Tax due at Standard Rate	K Cumulative Tax due at Higher Rate	L Cumulative Gross tax	M Cumulative Tax Credit	N Cumulative Tax (cannot be less than 0)	O Tax Deducted this Period	P Tax Refunded this Period
	€ c	€ c	€ c	€ c	€ c	€ c	€ c	€ c	€ c	€ c
1										
2										
3										
4										
5										
6										
7										
8										
9										
10										
11										
12										
13										
14										
15										
16										
17										
18										
19										
20										
21										
22										
23										
24										
25										
26										
27										
28										
29										
30										
31										
32										
33										
34										
35										
36										
37										
38										
39										
40										
41										
42										
43										
44										
45										
46										
47										
48										
49										
50										
51										
52										
53										

Previous Employment DEDUCT

← Pay

J6

← Pay

This Employment Net Tax deducted or Net Tax refunded

Tax →

J7

H9

Day Month Year

F4
F5

If employment ceased during the tax year enter date of cessation at F5

If employment began (a) in Week 1 or later or (b) before Week 1 but first pay day was in Week 1 or later, enter date of commencement at F4

FIGURE 3.2 OWN SYSTEM TAX DEDUCTION CARD

Employee Deduction Sheet

Name _____

Address _____

Employee Number _____

PPS Number _____

Commenced _____ Left _____

Date	Overtime / Commis. / Bonus	Gross Pay	Gross Less Pen/He	Cum Pay to Date	Cum Cut-Off Point	Cum Standard Tax	Cum Higher Tax	Cum Gross Tax	Cum Tax Credit	Cum Tax Due	Tax Refund	Employee Statutory Tax	Employee Statutory PRSI	Deductions Voluntary 1	Deductions Voluntary 2	Total Deduct.	Net Pay less Deduct.	Total PRSI	S.I. Week No

(Standard Pay column under Overtime/Commis./Bonus)

Cumulative Tax System and PRSI

Let's take a practical example to demonstrate how to complete an official cumulative TDC for the first few weeks of the tax year.

Example 3.6

Mary Ginty earns €450.00 gross per week. In weeks three and four she earned commission of €50.00 and €75.00 respectively. Her first pay day is 5 January. She pays a total of 5% towards superannuation and health benefit. Her cut-off point is €520.00 per week and her tax credit is €45.00 per week. She pays class A1 PRSI. For the solution, see Figure 3.3 below.

FIGURE 3.3 TAX DEDUCTION CARD FOR MARY GINTY

Wk No.	Gross Pay less Superann/ Health €	Cum Gross Pay to Date €	Cum Standard Rate Cut-Off Point €	Cum Tax due at Standard Rate €	Cum Tax due at Higher Rate €	Cum Gross Tax €	Cum Tax Credit €	Cum Tax (not less than 0) €	Tax Deduct this period €	Tax Refund this period €	PRSI EE €	PRSI Total €
1	427.50	427.50	520.00	85.50	0.00	85.50	45.00	40.50	40.50	0.00	20.57	66.53
2	427.50	855.00	1,040.00	171.00	0.00	171.00	90.00	81.00	40.50	0.00	20.57	66.53
3	475.00	1,330.00	1,560.00	266.00	0.00	266.00	135.00	131.00	50.00	0.00	23.42	4.48
4	498.75	1,828.75	2,080.00	365.75	0.00	365.75	180.00	185.75	54.75	0.00	24.85	78.47

An explanation of each of the column headings of the TDC follows.

Week No.

If an employee is paid in week number one, then pay day must be between 1 January and 7 January inclusive. Week number two is from 8 January to 14 January inclusive, and so on. Check the income tax calendar year in Appendix A.

Gross Pay Less Superannuation / Health

This is Mary's total pay (i.e. basic plus extras such as overtime, bonuses, etc.) after superannuation and health benefit (if any) are deducted. In fact this is called 'net pay'. To recap on the information on net pay, see Chapter 1 page 2.

Cumulative Gross Pay to Date

This is the combined or running total of her pay so far.

Cumulative Standard Rate Cut-Off Point

This is an amount of money which is liable for tax at the standard rate each week or month of the tax year. The tax office calculates the annual cut-off point figure and this is then divided into equal weekly or monthly amounts for the year. It accumulates during the year, so that by 31 December it amounts to the total annual cut-off point. The cut-off point varies from person to person depending on personal circumstances (see Chapter 2). The employer takes this figure from the (summary) tax credit certificate, which is provided by the tax office. If a TDC is issued by the tax office, the cut-off point for the employee is preprinted in this column for each week or month of the tax year.

Cumulative Tax due at Standard Rate

This is the amount of tax that Mary owes at the standard or lower rate of tax. The amount is calculated as follows:

- multiply the *lower* of the cumulative standard rate cut-off point figure or the cumulative gross pay to date figure, by the standard rate tax percentage.

For week one in this example it is €427.50 x 20% = €85.50.

Cumulative Tax due at Higher Rate

This is the amount of tax that Mary owes at the higher rate of tax. The amount is calculated as follows:

- subtract the cumulative standard rate cut-off point figure from the cumulative gross pay figure and
- multiply the result by the higher rate of tax.

In this example none of Mary's pay is liable for tax at the higher rate. This is because Mary's standard rate cut-off point exceeds her gross pay every week. In the next example (Example 3.7) tax is payable at both the lower and higher rates.

Cumulative Gross Tax

This is the sum of the two amounts of tax calculated at both the standard and higher rates. In week one in this example it is: €85.50 + €0.00 = €85.50

Cumulative Tax Credit

This is an amount of money which reduces a person's tax liability. This credit is deducted from the gross tax to arrive at the net tax payable. In this example it is €42.00 per week. Similarly to the cut-off point, the annual tax credit to which a person is entitled is calculated by the tax office. This figure is then divided into equal weekly or monthly amounts for the tax year. It accumulates during the year, so that by 31 December it amounts to the total annual tax credit. The annual tax credit varies from person to person as seen in Chapter 2. The employer takes this figure from the (summary) tax credit certificate, which is provided by the tax office. If a TDC is issued by the tax office, the tax credit for the employee is preprinted in this column for each week or month of the tax year. Tax credits are non-refundable. For example, where the gross tax on gross pay is, say, €150.00 and the tax credit is €200.00, the difference of €50.00 is not refunded. The employee simply has no tax liability for that period. The unused tax credit of €50.00 is carried forward and offset against future tax due on the cumulative basis.

Cumulative Tax

This is the amount of tax Mary owes for the year so far. It is calculated by deducting the cumulative tax credit from the cumulative gross tax. For week one in this example it is: €85.50 - €45.00 = €40.50. If the answer after deducting the cumulative tax credit from the cumulative gross tax was negative, then the cumulative tax would be *zero*.

Tax Deducted this period

This is the amount of tax that is deducted in an individual week or month. It is calculated by subtracting the *previous* week's or month's cumulative tax from the present week's or month's cumulative tax. In this example the cumulative tax due in week two is €81.00. In week one €40.50 was already deducted, therefore in week two €40.50 tax must be deducted, i.e. €81.00 - €40.50 = €40.50

Tax Refunded this period

If in any individual week or month the previous week's or month's cumulative tax is *greater* than the present week's or month's cumulative tax, then a refund is due to the employee. This is dealt with in Example 3.8 on pages 37–39.

PRSI

PRSI is calculated on the gross pay (less superannuation and permanent health benefit) figure each week or month. It is not a cumulative figure.

Mary's share of PRSI in week one is calculated as follows:

€127.00 x 2.0%	=	€2.54
€300.53 x 6.0%	=	€18.03
€427.50		€20.57

The employer's share is calculated as follows: €427.50 x 10.75% = €45.96.

The total PRSI contribution is €66.53 (i.e. €20.57 + €45.96). On the TDC, only the employee's share and the total PRSI contributions are recorded.

Insurable employment

A tick is marked each week or month that a PRSI contribution has been paid.

Example 3.7

William Clancy earns €650.00 gross per week. In week three he earned commission of €60.00. His first pay day is 6 January. His cut-off point is €520.00 per week and his tax credit is €47.00 per week. He pays class A1 PRSI. For the solution, see Figure 3.4 below.

FIGURE 3.4 TAX DEDUCTION CARD FOR WILLIAM CLANCY

Wk No.	Gross Pay less Superann/ Health €	Cum Gross Pay to Date €	Cum Standard Rate Cut-Off Point €	Cum Tax due at Standard Rate €	Cum Tax due at Higher Rate €	Cum Gross Tax €	Cum Tax Credit €	Cum Tax (not less than 0) €	Tax Deduct this period €	Tax Refund this period €	PRSI EE €	PRSI Total €
1	650.00	650.00	**520.00**	104.00	54.60	158.60	**47.00**	111.60	111.60	0.00	33.92	103.80
2	650.00	1,300.00	**1,040.00**	208.00	109.20	317.20	**94.00**	223.20	111.60	0.00	33.92	103.80
3	710.00	2,010.00	**1,560.00**	312.00	189.00	501.00	**141.00**	360.00	136.80	0.00	37.52	113.85
4	650.00	2,660.00	**2,080.00**	416.00	243.60	659.60	**188.00**	471.60	111.60	0.00	33.92	103.80

Note: In this example, tax is deducted at both the standard and higher rates. This is because William's gross pay exceeds his cut-off point, therefore he is taxed on the difference between these two amounts at the higher rate.

QUESTIONS ON THE CUMULATIVE TAX SYSTEM (FIRST SET)

The following three questions will give you some practice on the working of the cumulative tax system. Use the *current* rates of tax and PRSI in your calculations (see Appendices C and D). You may prefer to use the 'own system' TDC cards rather than the official ones. Use one of the TDCs in Appendix G (see Figure G.1 or Figure G.2).

> **Note 1:** The basic tax credits that an employee is entitled to are the Personal and PAYE credits.
> **Note 2:** The cut-off point is equivalent to the tax band.
> **Note 3:** Divide the annual credit and the cut-off point by fifty-two to get the weekly figure and by twelve to get the monthly figure.

Cumulative Tax System and PRSI

1. James Dolan, a single person, is taxed under the PAYE system. He pays 3% towards pension. He is entitled to the basic tax credits and cut-off point. He pays class A PRSI. His gross pay for the first five weeks of the tax year is as follows:
   - Week 1 €500
   - Week 2 €500
   - Week 3 €500
   - Week 4 €520
   - Week 5 €520

2. Debbie Nic Gabhann, a single person, is taxed under the PAYE system. She pays 3% towards pension. She is entitled to the basic tax credits and cut-off point. She pays class A PRSI. Her gross pay for the first five weeks of the tax year is as follows:
   - Week 1 €400
   - Week 2 €440
   - Week 3 €380
   - Week 4 €440
   - Week 5 €460

3. Sheena Buttimer, a single person, is taxed under the PAYE system. She is entitled to the basic tax credits and cut-off point. She pays class D PRSI. Her gross pay for the first five weeks of the tax year is as follows:
   - Week 1 €620
   - Week 2 €600
   - Week 3 €680
   - Week 4 €680
   - Week 5 €700

Example 3.8

Maeve Clancy's gross weekly earnings for seven weeks are as follows:

- Week 1 €445
- Week 2 €460
- Week 3 Nil (unofficial leave)
- Week 4 €445
- Week 5 €480
- Week 6 €100
- Week 7 €460

She pays a total of 5% towards pension and health benefit. Her cut-off point is €490.00 per week and her tax credit is €43.95 per week. She pays class A PRSI. For the solution see Figure 3.5.

FIGURE 3.5 TAX DEDUCTION CARD FOR MAEVE CLANCY

Wk No.	Gross Pay less Superann/ Health	Cum Gross Pay to Date	Cum Standard Rate Cut-Off Point	Cum Tax due at Standard Rate	Cum Tax due at Higher Rate	Cum Gross Tax	Cum Tax Credit	Cum Tax (not less than 0)	Tax Deduct this period	Tax Refund this period	PRSI EE	PRSI Total
	€	€	€	€	€	€	€	€	€	€	€	€
1	422.75	422.75	**490.00**	84.55	0.00	84.55	**43.95**	40.60	40.60	0.00	20.29	65.74
2	437.00	859.75	**980.00**	171.95	0.00	171.95	**87.90**	84.05	43.45	0.00	21.14	68.12
3	0.00	859.75*	**1,470.00**	171.95*	0.00	171.95	***131.85**	40.10	0.00	43.95*	0.00	0.00
4	422.75	1,282.50	**1,960.00**	256.50	0.00	256.50	**175.80**	80.70	40.60	0.00	20.29	65.74
5	456.00	1,738.50	**2,450.00**	347.70	0.00	347.70	**219.75**	127.95	47.25	0.00	22.28	71.30
6	95.00	1,833.50	**2,940.00**	366.70	0.00	366.70	**263.70**	103.00	0.00	24.95*	0.00	8.08
7	437.00	2,270.50	**3,430.00**	454.10	0.00	454.10	**307.65**	146.45	43.45	0.00	21.14	68.12

The entries marked with an (*) are explained below.

- **Cumulative Gross Pay in week three**
  The cumulative pay in this week is €859.75, the same as that in week two, because Maeve had no earnings in week three. Therefore, her cumulative pay remains unchanged for week three.

- **Cumulative Tax due at Standard Rate in week three**
  The cumulative tax due at the standard rate in week three is the same as that in week two. This is because there is no *extra* pay in week three which is liable for tax at the standard rate. Furthermore, the cumulative standard rate cut-off point is still greater than the cumulative gross pay to date. This means that none of Maeve's pay is liable for tax at the higher rate.

- **Cumulative Tax Credit in week three**
  Maeve is entitled to the tax credit of €43.95 in week three even though she doesn't work in that week. This is because the tax credit is an annual figure allowed in fifty-two equal amounts for the year.

- **Tax Refund in week three**
  This is because Maeve's gross tax in week three is the same as that in week two. However, she is entitled to her tax credit of €43.95 on a cumulative basis. In week three this has the effect of reducing the cumulative tax due in this week. In week two she owed €84.05 cumulative tax and by week three she owes only €40.10 tax. Therefore, she is entitled to a refund of the difference between the tax she owes to date and the tax she has paid to date. This is: €84.05 − €40.10 = €43.95. The refund can also be generated as follows:

Cumulative Tax System and PRSI 39

  Tax on €00.00 @ 20 % = €00.00
  Tax Credit = €43.95
  Tax Refund = €43.95

- **Tax Refund in week six**
  This situation is similar to that in week three. However, because Maeve had earnings in this week (though small) the cumulative tax due has increased. Again in week five she owed €127.95 cumulative tax and by week six she owes only €103.00. The difference between these two amounts results in a refund of €24.95. The refund can also be generated as follows:

  Tax on €95.00 @ 20 % = €19.00
  Tax Credit = €43.95
  Tax Refund = €24.95

Note: Any refund of tax due to an employee who has become unemployed will be made by the Revenue Commissioners on receipt of a completed form P50 and selected parts of the form P45.

QUESTIONS ON THE CUMULATIVE TAX SYSTEM (SECOND SET)

The following questions will give you more practice working on the cumulative tax system. You may prefer to use the 'own system' TDCs rather than the official ones.

Use the *current* rates of tax and PRSI in your calculations (see Appendices C and D).

1. Ellie Edmond, a married person, is taxed under the PAYE system. She is entitled to the basic tax credits and cut-off point, both divided equally between herself and her husband. She pays class A PRSI. Her gross pay for the first five weeks of the tax year is as follows:
   - Week 1 €600
   - Week 2 €550
   - Week 3 Nil (unofficial leave)
   - Week 4 €600
   - Week 5 €550

2. Susie Cunningham, a single person, is taxed under the PAYE system. She pays 5% towards pension. She is entitled to the basic tax credits and cut-off point. She pays class D PRSI. Her gross pay for the first five weeks of the tax year is as follows:
   - Week 1 €720
   - Week 2 €750
   - Week 3 Nil (unofficial leave)
   - Week 4 €720
   - Week 5 €770

HOLIDAYS

Holiday pay is earned against time worked. All employees, full-time, part-time, temporary or casual, earn holiday entitlements from the time work is commenced. The Organisation of Working Time Act provides that most employees are entitled to four weeks' annual holidays, with pro-rata entitlements for periods of employment of less than one year.

In order to qualify for four weeks' annual leave an employee

(a) must have worked for the employer for at least 117 hours in each calendar month or
(b) must have worked for the same employer for at least 1,365 hours during a 'leave year'.

Pro-rata entitlements in terms of a percentage of time worked apply to part-time workers.

The time at which annual leave may be taken is determined by the employer having regard to work requirements and to the need for the employee to avail of rest and recreation. The pay for annual leave must be given in advance.

The Organisation of Working Time Act also provides the following nine public holidays:

(i) 1 January (New Year's Day)
(ii) St. Patrick's Day
(iii) Easter Monday
(iv) the first Monday in May
(v) the first Monday in June
(vi) the first Monday in August
(vii) the last Monday in October
(viii) Christmas Day
(ix) St Stephen's Day.

In respect of each public holiday, an employee is entitled to:

(a) a paid day off on the holiday, or
(b) a paid day off within a month, or
(c) an extra day's annual leave, or
(d) an extra day's pay.

as the employer may decide.

Cumulative Tax System and PRSI

What Is the Position Regarding 'Holiday Pay'?

The tax credits and cut-off point to be used in the calculation of holiday pay paid in advance of the usual pay day are strictly those which relate to the income tax week or month in which it is paid. If, however, the effect of paying holiday pay in advance is that the employee receives the equivalent of two or three weeks pay in the same week and no pay in the following week, or weeks, the tax credits and cut-off point for those weeks may be taken into account in the calculation of tax due on the normal pay and holiday pay.

Example 3.9

Niamh Dolan is taxed under the PAYE system. She earns €400.00 per week. Her weekly cut-off point is €495.00 and her tax credit is €46.00. She takes two weeks' holidays from the week beginning 22 January (i.e. weeks 4 and 5). She receives her holiday pay in advance of her going on holidays. For the solution, see Figure 3.6.

FIGURE 3.6 TAX DEDUCTION CARD FOR NIAMH DOLAN

Wk No.	Gross Pay less Superann/ Health €	Cum Gross Pay to Date €	Cum Standard Rate Cut-Off Point €	Cum Tax due at Standard Rate €	Cum Tax due at Higher Rate €	Cum Gross Tax €	Cum Tax Credit €	Cum Tax (not less than 0) €	Tax Deduct this period €	Tax Refund this period €
1	400.00	400.00	495.00	80.00	00.00	80.00	46.00	34.00	34.00	00.00
2	400.00	800.00	990.00	160.00	00.00	160.00	92.00	68.00	34.00	00.00
3	1,200.00	2,000.00	2,475.00	400.00	00.00	400.00	230.00	170.00	102.00	00.00
4	00.00	00.00	00.00	Holidays		00.00	00.00	00.00	00.00	
5	00.00	00.00	00.00	Holidays		00.00	00.00	00.00	00.00	
6	400.00	2,400.00	2,970.00	480.00	00.00	480.00	276.00	204.00	34.00	00.00
7	400.00	2,800.00	3,465.00	560.00	00.00	560.00	322.00	238.00	34.00	00.00

QUESTIONS ON THE CUMULATIVE TAX SYSTEM (THIRD SET)

Use the current rates of tax and PRSI in your calculations (see Appendices C and D).

Note: Both employees are paid their holiday money in advance of going on holidays.

1. Sean Mooney, a married person, is taxed under the PAYE system. He is entitled to the basic tax credits and cut-off point, both divided equally between himself and his wife. He pays class A PRSI. His gross pay for the first five weeks of the tax year is as follows:

- Week 1 €630
- Week 2 €630
- Week 3 Holidays (annual leave)
- Week 4 Holidays (annual leave)
- Week 5 €630

2. Linda Morris, a married person, is taxed under the PAYE system. She is entitled to the basic tax credits and cut-off point, both divided equally between herself and her husband. She pays class B PRSI. Her gross pay for the first six weeks of the tax year is as follows:
   - Week 1 €520
   - Week 2 €520
   - Week 3 €520
   - Week 4 Holidays (annual leave)
   - Week 5 Holidays (annual leave)
   - Week 6 €575

Example 3.10

Aoife Dolan's gross monthly earnings for four months are as follows:

- Month 1 €2,800
- Month 2 €2,800
- Month 3 €3,000
- Month 4 €2,680

Her cut-off point is €2,300 per month and her tax credit is €196 per month. She pays class A1 PRSI. For the solution, see Figure 3.7.

FIGURE 3.7 TAX DEDUCTION CARD FOR AOIFE DOLAN

Mth No.	Gross Pay less Superann/ Health €	Cum Gross Pay to Date €	Cum Standard Rate Cut-Off Point €	Cum Tax due at Standard Rate €	Cum Tax due at Higher Rate €	Cum Gross Tax €	Cum Tax Credit €	Cum Tax (not less than 0) €	Tax Deduct this period €	Tax Refund this period €	PRSI EE €	PRSI Total €
1	2,800.00	2,800.00	2,300.00	460.00	210.00	670.00	130.00	540.00	540.00	0.00	145.96	446.96
2	2,800.00	5,600.00	4,600.00	920.00	420.00	1,340.00	260.00	1,080.00	540.00	0.00	145.96	446.96
3	3,000.00	8,600.00	6,900.00	1,380.00	714.00	2,094.00	390.00	1,704.00	624.00	0.00	157.96	480.46
4	2,680.00	11,280.00	9,200.00	1,840.00	873.60	2,713.60	520.00	2,193.60	489.60	0.00	138.76	426.86

Note: The PRSI-free amount is €551.00 per month.

Cumulative Tax System and PRSI   43

QUESTIONS ON THE CUMULATIVE TAX SYSTEM (FOURTH SET)

Use the current rates of tax and PRSI in your calculations (see Appendices C and D).

1. Michael Dolan, a single person, is taxed under the PAYE system. He is entitled to the basic tax credits and cut-off point. He pays class A PRSI. His gross pay for the first five months of the tax year is as follows:
   - Month 1 €2,670
   - Month 2 €2,450
   - Month 3 €2,670
   - Month 4 €1,850
   - Month 5 €1,700

2. Anne Shaw, a married person, is taxed under the PAYE system. She is entitled to the basic tax credits and the credit for a six-year-old handicapped daughter. The tax credit and the cut-off point are divided equally between herself and her husband. She pays class A PRSI. Her gross pay for the first five months of the tax year is as follows:
   - Month 1 €2,450
   - Month 2 €2,450
   - Month 3 €2,000
   - Month 4 €1,800
   - Month 5 €2,000

What Happens if an Employee Starts Work During the Tax Year?

An employee may start work during the tax year for two reasons:

- an employee starts work for the first time sometime after 1 January
- an employee leaves one job and starts work with a new employer.

The following two examples illustrate these two situations and how they are dealt with.

Example 3.11

Maria Buckley started work for the first time in February. Her first pay day was 8 February. Her gross earnings for the first number of weeks of the year are shown on the TDC overleaf. Her cut-off point is €540.00 per week and her tax credit is €46.00 per week.

Why does Maria not pay any tax until week ten?

You've probably guessed it. Maria's first payment was in week number six of the tax year (check the date on your income tax calendar: see Appendix A). However, her tax credit and cut-off point amounts started in week one and have been accumulating since then. Remember that these are annual figures divided by fifty-two if paid weekly. It is not until week ten that Maria's cumulative gross tax exceeds her cumulative tax credit. Therefore, she pays tax in that week and continues to do so in the following weeks. For the solution to this example, see Figure 3.8 below.

FIGURE 3.8 TAX DEDUCTION CARD FOR MARIA BUCKLEY

Wk No.	Gross Pay less Superann/ Health €	Cum Gross Pay to Date €	Cum Standard Rate Cut-Off Point €	Cum Tax due at Standard Rate €	Cum Tax due at Higher Rate €	Cum Gross Tax €	Cum Tax Credit €	Cum Tax (not less than 0) €	Tax Deduct this period €	Tax Refund this period €
1			540.00				46.00			
2			1,080.00				92.00			
3			1,620.00				138.00			
4			2,160.00				184.00			
5			2,700.00				230.00			
6	500.00	500.00	3,240.00	100.00	0.00	100.00	276.00	0.00	0.00	0.00
7	450.00	950.00	3,780.00	190.00	0.00	190.00	322.00	0.00	0.00	0.00
8	500.00	1,450.00	4,320.00	290.00	0.00	290.00	368.00	0.00	0.00	0.00
9	500.00	1,950.00	4,860.00	390.00	0.00	390.00	414.00	0.00	0.00	0.00
10	400.00	2,350.00	5,400.00	470.00	0.00	470.00	460.00	10.00	10.00	0.00
11	450.00	2,800.00	5,940.00	560.00	0.00	560.00	506.00	54.00	44.00	0.00
12	400.00	3,200.00	6,480.00	640.00	0.00	640.00	552.00	88.00	34.00	0.00
13	400.00	3,600.00	7,020.00	720.00	0.00	720.00	598.00	122.00	34.00	0.00
14	500.00	4,100.00	7,560.00	820.00	0.00	820.00	644.00	176.00	54.00	0.00
15										
16										
17										

Example 3.12

Denis Buckley left his old job and started work with his present employer. He received his form P45 from the previous employer (you will learn a lot more about this form later). The details from this form indicate the following:

- gross pay since 1 January is €5,000
- tax paid since 1 January is €705.00
- his cut-off point is €500.00 per week and his weekly tax credit is €45.00
- PRSI paid to date at class A1 shows the employee contribution of €256.70 and a total of €812.50.

Cumulative Tax System and PRSI

With his new employer, Denis is paid €560.00 (less pension) per week. His first pay day is 10 March. He pays class A PRSI.

The first few weeks with his new employer are recorded on the TDC; see Figure 3.9 below.

FIGURE 3.9 TAX DEDUCTION CARD FOR DENIS BUCKLEY

Wk No.	Gross Pay less Superann/ Health €	Cum Gross Pay to Date €	Cum Standard Rate Cut-Off Point €	Cum Tax due at Standard Rate €	Cum Tax due at Higher Rate €	Cum Gross Tax €	Cum Tax Credit €	Cum Tax (not less than 0) €	Tax Deduct this period €	Tax Refund this period €	PRSI EE €	PRSI Total €
1			500.00				45.00					
2			1,000.00				90.00					
3			1,500.00				135.00					
4			2,000.00				180.00					
5			2,500.00				225.00					
6			3,000.00				270.00					
7			3,500.00				315.00					
8			4,000.00				360.00					
9		5,000.00	4,500.00				405.00	705.00			256.70	812.50
10	560.00	5,560.00	5,000.00	1,000.00	235.20	1,235.20	450.00	785.20	80.20	0.00	28.52	88.72
11	560.00	6,120.00	5,500.00	1,100.00	260.40	1,360.40	495.00	865.40	80.20	0.00	28.52	88.72
12	560.00	6,680.00	6,000.00	1,200.00	285.60	1,485.60	540.00	945.60	80.20	0.00	28.52	88.72
13	560.00	7,240.00	6,500.00	1,300.00	310.80	1,610.80	585.00	1,025.80	80.20	0.00	28.52	88.72
14	560.00	7,800.00	7,000.00	1,400.00	336.00	1,736.00	630.00	1,106.00	80.20	0.00	28.52	88.72
15												
16												
17												

What Happens if an Employee's Tax Credit is Altered During the Tax Year?

An employee's tax credit certificate may be adjusted at any time during the year. It is the employer's duty to use the certificate with the most recent date on it. When the tax credit of an employee is amended the employer receives the information in one of the following ways:

- a revised official TDC is sent to the employer who is using the official manual TDC
- a revised tax credit certificate is sent to the employer using an 'own system' TDC
- a revised tax credit in electronic format is issued to the employer who is a member of the *Computer Media Exchange Scheme.*

The employer must transfer the following information from the old TDC to the corresponding columns on the new TDC.

1. The final entries on the old TDC for cumulative gross pay to date and cumulative tax.
2. The totals of the PRSI entries on the old TDC for the employee's contributions and for total contributions.

The employer must operate PAYE on the amended TDC from the next pay day. The employer must mark the old TDC *Transferred to new TDC*, and retain it with the new TDC.

Example 3.13

Shane Kelleher is paid €2,500 monthly. His annual cut-off point is €28,000. His tax credit was €2,350 (€195.83 per month) until he received an amended certificate showing an annual tax credit of €2,850 (€237.50 per month). The new certificate is effective from 5 June. The completion of both his old and new TDCs is shown in Figure 3.10 and Figure 3.11.

FIGURE 3.10 TAX DEDUCTION CARD (OLD VERSION) FOR SHANE KELLEHER

Mth No.	Gross Pay less Superann/ Health €	Cum Gross Pay to Date €	Cum Standard Rate Cut-Off Point €	Cum Tax due at Standard Rate €	Cum Tax due at Higher Rate €	Cum Gross Tax €	Cum Tax Credit €	Cum Tax (not less than 0) €	Tax Deduct this period €	Tax Refund this period €
1	2,500.00	2,500.00	**2,333.33**	466.67	70.00	536.67	**195.83**	340.84	340.84	0.00
2	2,500.00	5,000.00	**4,666.66**	933.33	140.00	1,073.33	**391.66**	681.67	340.84	0.00
3	2,500.00	7,500.00	**6,999.99**	1,400.00	210.00	1,610.00	**587.49**	1,022.51	340.84	0.00
4	2,500.00	10,000.00	**9,333.32**	1,866.67	280.00	2,146.67	**783.32**	1,363.35	340.84	0.00
5	2,500.00	12,500.00	**11,666.65**	2,333.33	350.00	2,683.33	**979.15**	1,704.18	340.84	0.00
					Transferred to new TDC					
Totals	12,500.00							1,704.18		

FIGURE 3.11 TAX DEDUCTION CARD (NEW VERSION) FOR SHANE KELLEHER

Mth No.	Gross Pay less Superann/ Health €	Cum Gross Pay to Date €	Cum Standard Rate Cut-Off Point €	Cum Tax due at Standard Rate €	Cum Tax due at Higher Rate €	Cum Gross Tax €	Cum Tax Credit €	Cum Tax (not less than 0) €	Tax Deduct this period €	Tax Refund this period €
1			2,333.33				237.50			
2			4,666.66				475.00			
3			6,999.99	*Transferred from old TDC*			712.50			
4			9,333.32				950.00			
5		12,500.00	11,666.65				1,187.50	1,704.18		
6	2,500.00	15,000.00	13,999.98	2,800.00	420.00	3,220.00	1,425.00	1,795.00	90.82	0.00
7	2,500.00	17,500.00	16,333.33	3,266.67	490.00	3,756.67	1,662.50	2,094.17	299.17	0.00
8	2,500.00	20,000.00	18,666.65	3,733.33	560.00	4,293.33	1,900.00	2,393.33	299.17	0.00
9	2,500.00	22,500.00	21,000.00	4,200.00	630.00	4,830.00	2,137.50	2,692.50	299.17	0.00
10	2,500.00	25,000.00	21,333.33	4,666.67	700.00	5,366.67	2,375.00	2,991.67	299.17	0.00
11	2,500.00	27,500.00	25,666.67	5,133.33	770.00	5,903.33	2,612.50	3,290.83	299.17	0.00
12	2,500.00	30,000.00	28,000.00	5,600.00	840.00	6,440.00	2,850.00	3,590.00	299.17	0.00

QUESTIONS ON THE CUMULATIVE TAX SYSTEM (FIFTH SET)

Complete the TDCs for the following two employees for the tax year, showing the effect of a change in the tax credit during the tax year. Use the current rates of tax and PRSI in your calculations (see Appendices C and D).

1. John Redmond, a married person, is paid €2,500 monthly. He is entitled to the basic tax credits and cut-off point. He had omitted to claim the incapacitated child credit at the beginning of the tax year. He contacted his tax office and was issued with a new tax credit certificate. The new certificate is effective from 2 June. All credits are shared equally with his wife. He pays class A PRSI.

2. Helen O' Neill, a married person, is paid €3,000 monthly. She is entitled to the basic tax credits and cut-off point. She had omitted to claim the incapacitated child credit at the beginning of the tax year. She contacted her tax office and was issued with a new tax credit certificate. The new certificate is effective from 3 April. All credits are shared equally with her husband. She pays class A PRSI.

QUESTIONS ON THE CUMULATIVE TAX SYSTEM (SIXTH SET)

Use the current rates of tax and PRSI in your calculations (see Appendices C and D). You will find the 'own system' TDCs more appropriate for answering these questions.

You have started work in the payroll department of a local firm. Your first task is to complete the TDCs for week ten and for the next three weeks. All the relevant details to process the payroll are supplied for each employee in the table below.

Name	Anne Kelly €	Mary Lane €	John Ryan €	Tim Taylor €
Gross basic pay (less pension)	650.00	435.00	378.00	625.00
Gross pay year to date	5,850.00	3,915.00	3,402.00	5,625.00
Tax paid to date	967.95	352.80	284.40	841.95
Weekly cut-off point	540.00	539.00	541.00	530.00
Weekly tax credit	46.65	47.80	44.00	52.35
PRSI class	A	B	A	A

Note the following points:

- All employees pay €12.00 per week union dues (i.e. non-statutory deduction).
- Anne Kelly and Tim Taylor also pay €35.00 each per week to the staff credit union.
- John Ryan earned a bonus of €45.00 in week eleven and €52.00 in week thirteen.
- Tim Taylor receives a benefit-in-kind worth €42.50 per week.
- Mary Lane's annual tax credit was adjusted from the current one of €2,485 to €2,600, i.e. from €47.80 per week to €51.75, and this is effective from week twelve onwards.

Chapter 4

Emergency and Temporary Tax Systems

In this chapter you will learn:

- the terminology associated with the emergency and temporary tax systems
- why an individual may be taxed under these systems
- how to complete the emergency TDC and temporary TDC (Form P13/P14).

EMERGENCY TAX

When an employee commences employment, the employer must notify the Inspector of Taxes and apply for a TDC in the employee's name. An employee may be placed on the emergency tax system for any one of the following three reasons:

- the employer has not received, in respect of the employee, either a tax credit certificate or a TDC for the current year or a form P45 for the current or previous tax year for the employee

or

- the employee has given the employer a completed form P45 indicating that the employee is on emergency tax. This is shown on line 4 of the form. Figure 4.1 on pages 51 and 52 shows a sample Emergency TDC

or

- the employee has given the employer a completed form P45 without a PPS number, while not indicating that the emergency basis applies.

Typically, a school leaver or someone starting work for the first time is placed on the emergency system for a certain period.

How Does the Emergency Tax System Operate?

For employees who have a PPS number, a provisional cut-off point and tax credit are given for a number of weeks or months of employment. The employee's cut-off point and tax credit are calculated as one fifty-second of these figures if paid weekly and one-twelfth if paid monthly. The amounts are fixed and non-cumulative. The standard and higher rates of tax apply to the taxable income. For employees without a PPS number, all of their income is taxed at the higher rate.

An employee remains on the emergency tax system until he or she obtains a tax credit certificate and the employer has also been notified of the change. The employee is then transferred to the cumulative tax system, effective in the next pay week or month.

FIGURE 4.1 AN OFFICIAL EMERGENCY TDC

Revenue — Temporary/Emergency Tax Deduction Card
*For the Tax Year Ended 31 December 200_*

EMPLOYER'S Name & Address

Employer's Number
EMPLOYEE DETAILS
PPS Number   Works Number (N6)
Name   Period
Standard Tax Rate: 20%   Higher Tax Rate: 42%

This Tax Deduction Card (TDC) can be used as an Emergency TDC or a Temporary TDC

Used as Emergency Card ☐   Used as a Temporary Card ☐

Use this as an Emergency TDC when:
- You have **not** received either a certificate of Tax Credits and Standard Rate Cut-Off Point or a form P45 for the current year, **or**
- You receive a P45 from an employee which indicates that emergency tax applied in the previous employment, or
- The employee has given the employer a completed P45 without a PPS number and not indicating that the emergency basis applies.

Tax is calculated on the gross pay (after deduction of pension contributions and permanent health contributions where relevant). Different rules apply depending on whether or not the employee provides an employer with his/her PPS number.

The tables below outline the tax credits and cut-off points applicable.

The standard rate of tax is 20%. The higher rate of tax is 42%

Employee does not provide a PPS Number

Week or Month	Cut-Off Point	Tax Credit
All	0.00	0.00

Employee does provide a PPS Number

Weekly Paid	Cut-Off Point	Tax Credit
Week 1 to 4		
Week 5 to 8		
Week 9 onwards		

Monthly Paid	Cut-Off Point	Tax Credit
Month 1		
Month 2		
Month 3 onwards		

Where for example an employee starts employment without a PPS Number, provides it in say week 3, but still has not provided a P45 or Tax Credit Certificate, tax should be applied at Week 3 per the schedule listed above and continued into Week 4 and 5 etc., as appropriate, until such time as a P45 or Tax Credit Certificate is provided.

Use this as a Temporary TDC when:
- You have received a P45 from an employee which indicates the Tax Credits and Standard Rate Cut-Off Point to be used.

Detailed notes on relevant entries are included overleaf.

P13/P14

A Date of Payment	B See PAYE Calendar (Month / Week)	C PRSI Employee's Share	D PRSI Total contribution	E Social Ins weekly record
	1 Jan. to 31 Jan — 1,2,3,4			
	1 Feb. to 28 Feb — 5,6,7,8,9			
	1 Mar. to 31 Mar — 10,11,12,13			
	1 Apr. to 30 Apr — 14,15,16,17,18			
	1 May to 31 May — 19,20,21,22			
	1 June to 30 June — 23,24,25,26			
	1 July to 31 July — 27,28,29,30,31			
	1 Aug. to 31 Aug — 32,33,34,35			
	1 Sept. to 30 Sept — 36,37,38,39			
	1 Oct. to 31 Oct — 40,41,42,43,44			
	1 Nov. to 30 Nov — 45,46,47,48			
	1 Dec. to 31 Dec — 49,50,51,52,53			
	K3			Total Weeks
	K4		F2	

Social Insurance Class
C2 ☐   Initial Class
IF Class changed during this employment complete these boxes
B4 ___   Date of Change ___   C3 ___ Other Class   F3 ___ Weeks at Other Class

N.B. If more than two classes please furnish details on Form PRC 1

Emergency and Temporary Tax Systems

Week No.	F Gross Pay (Less Superannuation) This Period		G Standard Rate Cut-Off Point This Period		H Tax Due at Standard Rate This Period		I Tax Due at Higher Rate This Period		J Gross Tax This Period		K Tax Credit This Period		L Tax Due this Period		M For Employer Use		Description of Entry for each Column
	€	c	€	c	€	c	€	c	€	c	€	c	€	c	€	c	
1																	**Column C, D, E** PRSI Details
2																	
3																	
4																	
5																	
6																	**Column F** Gross pay: (Including overtime, bonus, commissions etc.) after deduction of any Superannuation and contributions to a Revenue Approved permanent health benefit scheme payable and allowable for income tax purposes.
7																	
8																	
9																	
10																	
11																	
12																	
13																	
14																	
15																	
16																	
17																	
18																	**Column G** Temporary TDC: Standard rate cut-off point as shown on Form P45. Emergency TDC: See notes overleaf
19																	
20																	
21																	
22																	
23																	
24																	
25																	
26																	**Column H** Tax due at standard rate of tax this period
27																	
28																	
29																	
30																	**Column I** Tax due at higher rate of tax this period
31																	
32																	
33																	
34																	**Column J** Gross tax this period
35																	
36																	
37																	**Column K** Temporary TDC: Tax credits as shown on Form P45. Emergency TDC: See notes overleaf
38																	
39																	
40																	
41																	
42																	
43																	
44																	**Column L** Tax due for this period
45																	
46																	**Column M** Freeflow e.g., net pay, employer's PRSI etc.
47																	
48																	
49																	
50																	
51																	
52																	
53																	

J6 ← Pay   Tax → J7

Day Month Year

F4
F5

If employment ceased during the tax year enter date of cessation at F5

If employment began
(a) in Week 1 or later, or
(b) before Week 1 but first pay day was in Week 1 or later, enter date of commencement at F4

Table 4.1 and Table 4.2 show the cut-off points and tax credits for employees with and without PPS numbers. You may insert the details yourself for the current tax year in the columns provided.

TABLE 4.1 EMERGENCY TAX CUT-OFF POINTS AND TAX CREDITS IN A SAMPLE TAX YEAR FOR EMPLOYEES WITH A PPS NUMBER

Weekly Paid	Cut-off Point €	Tax Credit €	Current Year Cut-off Point €	Tax Credit €
Week 1 to 4	540	30.00		
Week 5 to 8	540	Nil		
Week 9 onwards	Nil	Nil		
Monthly Paid	Cut-off Point €	Tax Credit €	Current Year Cut-off Point €	Tax Credit €
Month 1	2,334	127		
Month 2	2,334	Nil		
Month 3 onwards	Nil	Nil		

TABLE 4.2 EMERGENCY TAX CUT-OFF POINTS AND TAX CREDITS IN A SAMPLE TAX YEAR FOR EMPLOYEES WITHOUT A PPS NUMBER

Weekly Paid	Cut-off Point €	Tax Credit €	Current Year Cut-off Point €	Tax Credit €
All	Nil	Nil		

Note: The first 'week or month of employment' doesn't necessarily have to correspond with the first week or month of the tax year. For example, if the first pay day for an employee (weekly paid) is on 4 September which is week number thirty-six of the tax year, then this is the 'first' week of employment and the rules as listed in Table 4.1 apply. However, if the first pay day is on 5 January, then the 'first' week corresponds to the first week of the tax year.

It is at the employee's discretion to come off the emergency system. For example, students in summer jobs may choose to stay on the emergency system for the duration of their employment. The large amount of tax paid acts as a saving, because they will be entitled to a refund when they cease work or come off the emergency system.

There are *no refunds* if tax is overpaid while an employee is on emergency tax. Any overpayment of tax will be refunded when the cumulative basis of tax is applied. Like the cumulative tax system, the tax office will pay any refund due to an employee who has become unemployed. The employee must apply for a refund to the Inspector of Taxes with a completed form P50 and parts two and three of the form P45.

When a cumulative TDC replaces the emergency TDC, the information from the emergency TDC must be transferred to the cumulative TDC. The cumulative TDC must be marked: *Non-Cumulative Basis*. The emergency TDC must be marked *Transferred to new TDC*. Both cards must be kept on file. The information transferred includes the following:

- gross pay (less superannuation and health benefit) to date
- total tax deducted to date
- employee's share of PRSI paid to date
- total PRSI contribution paid to date.

Example 4.1

Sean Flood (PPS 5487995K) started work for the first time. His first pay day was 5 January. He did not have a tax credit certificate and he was placed on emergency tax. He spent ten weeks on this system. He was paid €400.00 per week. The completion of Sean's emergency TDC is shown in Figure 4.2.

FIGURE 4.2 EMERGENCY TDC FOR SEAN FLOOD

Wk No.	Gross less Superann / Health €	Standard Rate Cut-Off Point €	Tax at Standard Rate €	Tax at Higher Rate €	Gross Tax €	Credit Tax €	Tax Deducted in Week €
1	400.00	**540.00**	80.00	00.00	80.00	**30.00**	50.00
2	400.00	**540.00**	80.00	00.00	80.00	**30.00**	50.00
3	400.00	**540.00**	80.00	00.00	80.00	**30.00**	50.00
4	400.00	**540.00**	80.00	00.00	80.00	**30.00**	50.00
5	400.00	**540.00**	80.00	00.00	80.00	**00.00**	80.00
6	400.00	**540.00**	80.00	00.00	80.00	**00.00**	80.00
7	400.00	**540.00**	80.00	00.00	80.00	**00.00**	80.00
8	400.00	**540.00**	80.00	00.00	80.00	**00.00**	80.00
9	400.00	**0.00**	00.00	168.00	168.00	**00.00**	168.00
10	400.00	**0.00**	00.00	168.00	168.00	**00.00**	168.00

Example 4.2

Nora Keane (PPS 1478335J) started work in February for the first time. She was paid €300.00 per week. Her first pay day was 2 February. She didn't have a tax credit certificate and was placed on emergency tax. She spent seven weeks on this system. The following week, she was transferred to the cumulative tax system. Her tax credit certificate, effective from week eight, contained the following details:

- cut-off point €540.00 per week
- tax credit €45.00 per week.

To view the solution, see Figure 4.3 and Figure 4.4.

FIGURE 4.3 EMERGENCY TDC FOR NORA KEANE

Wk No.	Gross less Superann / Health €	Standard Rate Cut-Off Point €	Tax at Standard Rate €	Tax at Higher Rate €	Gross Tax €	Credit Tax €	Tax Deducted in Week
1							
2							
3							
4							
5	300.00	**540.00**	60.00	00.00	60.00	**30.00**	30.00
6	300.00	**540.00**	60.00	00.00	60.00	**30.00**	30.00
7	300.00	**540.00**	60.00	00.00	60.00	**30.00**	30.00
8	300.00	**540.00**	60.00	00.00	60.00	**30.00**	30.00
9	300.00	**540.00**	60.00	00.00	60.00	**00.00**	60.00
10	300.00	**540.00**	60.00	00.00	60.00	**00.00**	60.00
11	300.00	**540.00**	60.00	00.00	60.00	**00.00**	60.00
12							
13							
			Transferred to new TDC				
Total	2,100.00						300.00

Emergency and Temporary Tax Systems

FIGURE 4.4 CUMULATIVE TDC FOR NORA KEANE

Wk No.	Gross Pay less Superann/ Health €	Cum Gross Pay to Date €	Cum Standard Rate Cut-Off Point €	Cum Tax due at Standard Rate €	Cum Tax due at Higher Rate €	Cum Gross Tax €	Cum Tax Credit €	Cum Tax (not less than 0) €	Tax Deduct this period €	Tax Refund this period €
1			540.00				45.00			
2			1,080.00				90.00			
3			1,620.00				135.00			
4			2,160.00				180.00			
5			2,700.00				225.00			
6			3,240.00	*Non-Cumulative Basis*			270.00			
7			3,780.00				315.00			
8			4,320.00				360.00			
9			4,860.00				405.00			
10			5,400.00				450.00			
11		2,100.00	5,940.00				495.00	300.00		
12	300.00	2,400.00	6,480.00	480.00	00.00	480.00	540.00	00.00	00.00	300.00
13	300.00	2,700.00	7,020.00	540.00	00.00	540.00	585.00	00.00	00.00	00.00
14	300.00	3,000.00	7,560.00	600.00	00.00	600.00	630.00	00.00	00.00	00.00
15	500.00	3,500.00	8,100.00	700.00	00.00	700.00	675.00	25.00	25.00	00.00
16										
17										
18										
19										

QUESTIONS ON EMERGENCY TAX

Answer the following questions using the current rates of tax and PRSI in your calculations (see Appendices C and D).

1. Sharon McCabe (PPS 4756478L) started work in January for the first time earning €560.00 per week. The first pay day was 5 January. She did not have a tax credit certificate and was placed on emergency tax. She spent nine weeks on this system. Complete the emergency TDC using the one in Figure G.3 in Appendix G.

2. Paul Heffernan (PPS 4789632M) started work in February for the first time earning €420.00 per week. The first pay day was 3 February. He didn't have a tax credit certificate and was placed on emergency tax. He spent eight weeks on this system. The following week he was transferred to the cumulative tax system after

receiving his tax credit certificate. The details on this certificate included the following:

- cut-off point €542.00 per week
- tax credit €47.50 per week.

Complete the emergency TDC for the first eight weeks and the cumulative TDC for the following three weeks. Use the emergency TDC (see Figure G.3), and the cumulative TDC (see Figure G.1) in Appendix G.

3. Olan Callanan has no PPS number. He started work in March for the first time earning €380.00 per week. The first pay day was 4 March. He didn't have a tax credit certificate and was placed on emergency tax. He spent eight weeks on this system. Complete the emergency TDC using the one in Figure F.3 in Appendix G.

4. Frank Mc Morrow (PPS 4578110G) started work in April for the first time earning €300.00 per week. The first pay day was 22 April. He didn't have a tax credit certificate and was placed on emergency tax. He spent seven weeks on this system. The following week he was transferred to the cumulative tax system after receiving his tax credit certificate. The details on this certificate included the following:

- cut-off point €540.00 per week
- tax credit €46.95 per week.

Complete the emergency TDC for the first seven weeks and the cumulative TDC for the following three weeks.

5. Helen Jordan (PPS 11789632A) started work in May for the first time earning €420.00 per week. The first pay day was 2 May. She didn't have a tax credit certificate and was placed on emergency tax. She spent nine weeks on this system. The following week she was transferred to the cumulative tax system after receiving her tax credit certificate. The details on this certificate included the following:

- cut-off point €540.00 per week
- tax credit €45.95 per week.

Complete the emergency TDC for the first nine weeks and the cumulative TDC for the following three weeks.

TEMPORARY TAX

When an employee starts employment and until he or she is placed on the cumulative system, he or she may be placed on the temporary tax system for a period. The reasons for this may include the following:

- the employer is waiting for the cumulative TDC from the Inspector of Taxes
- an employee starts work during the tax year after being unemployed for a period
- an employee's tax is not up to date.

In such circumstances, the Inspector of Taxes directs an employer to deduct tax on a 'week one/month one' basis; that is, tax is deducted on a non-cumulative basis. This instruction will be clearly printed on the tax credit certificate or TDC. When a TDC is issued, the weekly cut-off point and the tax credit will be preprinted on the card for each of the income tax weeks of the year. The same applies for the TDC issued with a monthly cut-off point and tax credit.

If the 'week one/month one' basis applies, none of the pay, the cut-off point, or the tax credit is accumulated for tax purposes. The pay for each income tax week or month is dealt with separately. Likewise, the cut-off point and tax credit for each individual week or month is applied separately and tax is deducted accordingly.

There are no refunds under temporary tax. Pay is not accumulated for tax purposes. However, for PRSI contributions the employer must take into account the total pay to date, because of the income ceiling for the employee's PRSI contribution.

Similarly to the emergency tax system, when a TDC showing information on a non-cumulative basis (temporary) is replaced by one showing information on a cumulative basis, the information on the temporary TDC must be transferred to the cumulative TDC.

The temporary TDC must be marked: *Transferred to new TDC*. And the cumulative TDC is to be marked: *Non-Cumulative Basis*. The information transferred is identical to that which applied to the emergency system. To find out what information is transferred, see page 53 of this chapter.

Example 4.3

Seamus O'Malley started work in January, and his first pay day was 5 January. He earns €375.00 per week. He spent five weeks on the temporary tax system. The following week, he was transferred to the cumulative system. His tax credit certificate contained the following:

- cut-off point €540.00 per week
- tax credit €45.00 per week.

To view the solution, see Figure 4.4 and Figure 4.5.

FIGURE 4.5 TEMPORARY TDC FOR SEAMUS O'MALLEY

Wk No.	Gross less Superann / Health €	Cut-Off Point €	Tax at Standard Rate €	Tax at Higher Rate €	Gross Tax €	Credit Tax €	Tax Deducted in Week €
1	375.00	**540.00**	75.00	0.00	75.00	**45.00**	30.00
2	375.00	**540.00**	75.00	0.00	75.00	**45.00**	30.00
3	375.00	**540.00**	75.00	0.00	75.00	**45.00**	30.00
4	375.00	**540.00**	75.00	0.00	75.00	**45.00**	30.00
5	375.00	**540.00**	75.00	0.00	75.00	**45.00**	30.00
6							
7							
8							
9							
10			*Transferred to new TDC*				
11							
12							
13							
14							
15	1,875.00		150.00				

FIGURE 4.6 CUMULATIVE TDC FOR SEAMUS O'MALLEY

Wk No.	Gross Pay less Superann/ Health €	Cum Gross Pay to Date €	Cum Standard Rate Cut-Off Point €	Cum Tax due at Standard Rate €	Cum Tax due at Higher Rate €	Cum Gross Tax €	Cum Tax Credit €	Cum Tax (not less than 0) €	Tax Deduct this period €	Tax Refund this period €
1			**540.00**				**45.00**			
2			**1,080.00**				**90.00**			
3			**1,620.00**	*Non-Cumulative Basis*			**135.00**			
4			**2,160.00**				**180.00**			
5		1,875.00	**2,700.00**				**225.00**	150.00		
6	375.00	2,250.00	**3,240.00**	*450.00*	*00.00*	*450.00*	**270.00**	180.00	30.00	0.00
7	375.00	2,625.00	**3,780.00**	525.00	00.00	525.00	**315.00**	210.00	30.00	0.00
8	375.00	3,000.00	**4,320.00**	600.00	00.00	600.00	**360.00**	240.00	30.00	0.00
9										
10										
11										
12										

Emergency and Temporary Tax Systems

QUESTIONS ON TEMPORARY TAX

Use the current rates of tax and PRSI in your calculations (see Appendices C and D). Complete the temporary TDC and the first *two* weeks of the cumulative TDC for the following two employees.

Use the Temporary TDC in Appendix G (see Figure G.3). Use the cumulative TDC in Appendix G (see Figure G.1).

1. Deirdre McKenzie started work in February and her first pay day was 3 February. She earns €420.00 per week. She spent four weeks on the temporary tax system. The following week, she was transferred to the cumulative system. Her tax credit certificate contained the following information:

    - cut-off point €543.75 per week
    - tax credit €46.20 per week.

2. Kevin Nolan started work in April and his first pay day was 4 April. He earns €360.00 per week. He spent four weeks on the temporary tax system. The following week, he was transferred to the cumulative system. His tax credit certificate contained the following information:

    - cut-off point €540.00 per week
    - tax credit €45.00 per week.

Chapter 5

Tax Return Forms

In this chapter you will learn:

- the purpose of the main tax return forms: P30, P45, P60, P35L and P35
- how to complete these forms from data supplied.

Employers spend quite an amount of time completing payroll records on behalf of the Revenue Commissioners, so the end of the tax year is a particularly busy time for them. The officers of the Revenue Commissioners are empowered to inspect an employer's records at any time to ensure that the correct amounts of tax are being deducted, or have been deducted, and paid to the Revenue.

The employer must retain all documents and records relating to the calculation or payment of pay, or the deduction of tax or calculation of PRSI contributions (wages sheets, TDCs etc.) for *six years* after the end of the tax year to which they refer. However, they may be retained for a shorter period if notified in writing by the Revenue Commissioners. Such documents must be available for inspection by an authorised officer of the Revenue Commissioners.

Two of the main documents that an employer uses during the tax year are as follows:

- form P30 – Employer's remittance form (income tax and PRSI contributions)
- form P45 – Cessation certificate, which comprises four parts.

FORM P30 – EMPLOYER'S REMITTANCE FORM

A monthly remittance for PAYE tax and PRSI contributions must be sent to the Collector-General with a completed form P30 bank giro/payslip (see Figure 5.1). If the monthly remittance is likely to be a small amount, permission may be given to remit less frequently than once a month.

Payment to the Collector-General

The monthly remittance (form P30) must be sent to the Collector-General within *fourteen* days of the end of the income tax month during which the deductions were made. For example, the first remittance of the tax year will be due on 14 February at the latest.

Tax Return Forms

FIGURE 5.1 FORM P30 – EMPLOYER'S REMITTANCE FORM

In all Correspondence Please quote
Registration No: 1234567A

Notice No.: 1234567-00001A

MR BARNEY RUBBLE
C/O FLINTSTONES & CO
COBBLESTONE PLACE
BEDROCK
CO DUBLIN

Office of the Revenue Commissioners
Collector-Generals Division
Sarsfield House
Francis Street
Limerick

Enquiries: 1890203070

INCOME TAX (PAYE), SOCIAL INSURANCE, CONTRIBUTIONS AND LEVIES (PRSI)

Please see notes overleaf regarding completion and method of payment.

Period:
Payment due not later than:

These amounts are your own record of PAYE/PRSI remitted. These details must also be entered in the boxes on the payslip below.

	€
PAYE	
PRSI	
TOTAL	

€ (Currency)

Please do not photocopy this form or payslip or use it for any other period or customer.
Always return the payslip even for nil returns.

BANK GIRO CREDIT TRANSFER   **Payslip**   **P30**   **Revenue**

Name: MR BARNEY RUBBLE
Period:
I declare that the amount shown below is the amount I am liable to remit to the Collector-General for the above period.

Signed: _____ Date: _____

Registration No: 1234567A
Notice No: 1234567-00001A
Date Rec'd

	€	
PAYE		00
PRSI		00
TOTAL		00

Whole Euros only. Please do not enter cents.

Receiving Cashier's Brand & Initials.

CHEQUES	
TOTAL €	

Please do not fold this payslip or write or mark below this line.

P30 (EUR)

⑈90⑈7104⑆ 9328844⑈ 71

Method of Payment

Each registered employer is issued each month with a form P30 bank giro/payslip on which his or her name, address, registration number and the relevant month are printed.

The figures for total tax and total PRSI contributions must be entered on the form, together with the grand total, which equals the amount of the remittance.

The tax must always be kept separate from the PRSI contributions. The amounts received by the Collector-General for PRSI contributions are transferred to the Department of Social, Community and Family Affairs. The amounts received by the Collector-General for PAYE tax are transferred to the Department of Finance.

Payment may be made in any of the following ways:

- by lodging the total amount due, with the completed bank giro/payslip, at any bank
- by sending a cheque for the total amount due, with the completed bank giro/payslip, to the Collector-General, Sarsfield Hse, Francis St, Limerick
- by direct debit through the banking system
- through the on-line direct debit service operated by **www.ros.ie**. This service has been available since 29 September 2000. It is a requirement that intending filers (e-filers) of P30s must complete a ROS Debit Instruction (RDI), giving the details of a bank account from which Revenue can collect the appropriate amount due at the due date.

Because each form P30 is specially coded for a particular month, it must *not* be used to accompany a payment for another month or a payment for more than one month.

What if No Tax or PRSI is Due?

In this instance, the employer must notify the Collector-General within fourteen days of the end of that month. The form P30 must be returned with *Nil* marked in the money columns for both PAYE and PRSI.

> **Note:**
> If the Revenue Commissioners believe that an employer who was liable to pay tax and/or PRSI contributions for any month or year has not paid any amount or has paid an insufficient amount, they are entitled to make an estimate of the amounts due. The employer will be served with a notice of the estimate. The employer has the right to appeal to the Appeal Commissioners.

Interest on Overdue Payments

The employer will be charged interest on any overdue payment (1.25% per month at present) for each month or part of a month for which payment is overdue. The minimum charge for each late payment is €6.50.

Separate Registration Remittances

An employer may have more than one registration number, so this means that a separate remittance must be returned for each registration number.

FORM P45 – CESSATION CERTIFICATE

When an employee leaves the employment (including dismissal), is granted a career break, or dies, the employer must complete a form P45. Figure 5.2 shows a form P45.

The form comes in four parts (carbonised). You must ensure that each part is legible when completing it. The purpose of each part is as follows.

- Part 1 – the employer must send this part to the tax office to inform the Revenue Commissioners that the taxpayer named on the form ceases to be his or her employee.
- Part 2 – the employer gives this part to the employee (along with parts 3 and 4, all attached together). If the employee takes up employment elsewhere, the employee hands parts 2 and 3 to the new employer. The employer keeps part 2, and uses the information supplied on the form to deduct tax and PRSI accordingly.
- Part 3 – the employer sends this part to the Revenue Commissioners. It acts as notification that the named taxpayer is a new employee and as a request for a TDC for this employee.
- Part 4 – a person who becomes unemployed uses this part to claim unemployment benefit from the Department of Social and Family Affairs.

The Revenue On-Line Service (ROS) provides a facility for the submission of part 1 of the P45 on-line and the printing of parts 2, 3 and 4 onto computer stationery, which is available from the Revenue Forms and Leaflets service.

If an employee dies, all four parts are returned to the Revenue Commissioners.

An employer must *not* under any circumstances supply duplicates of parts 2, 3 or 4 to an employee who has left the employment and claims to have lost the originals.

FIGURE 5.2 FORM P45

FORM P45
CERTIFICATE NO. **U683377**
INCOME TAX - PAY AS YOU EARN - CESSATION CERTIFICATE
Particulars of Employee Leaving

PLEASE COMPLETE FORM IN BLOCK CAPITALS

Surname
First Name(s)
Unit Number
PPS Number
Date of Leaving
Address
Date of Birth
Employer Registered Number
Payroll/Works No.
Deceased (Tick ✔ if applicable)
Commencement

○ Weekly   ○ Monthly (Please tick ✔ if you are paid weekly or Monthly)

Weekly/Monthly Tax Credit
Week/Month Number
Weekly/Monthly Standard Rate Cut-Off Point
Tick ✔ if emergency tax operated

(a) **TOTAL PAY & TAX** deducted from 1 January last to date of leaving
Total Pay   Total Tax Deducted

(b) If Employment commenced since 1 January last enter Pay and Tax deducted for this period of employment only
Pay   Tax Deducted

(c) Amount of Taxable **LUMP SUM PAYMENT** on termination included in either pay figure above - if applicable

(a) Total amount of Taxable Disability Benefit included in Total Pay above
(b) Amount by which Tax Credits were reduced
Amount by which Standard Rate Cut-Off Point was reduced
(c) Indicate that Week 1/Month 1 basis was applied (Tick ✔ if applicable)

Please complete **A,B or C** across where an employee was in receipt of taxable Disability Benefit since 1st January last while employed by you

PRSI - THIS EMPLOYMENT ONLY
Total PRSI
Employee's Share
Total number of weeks of Insurable Employment
Total number of weeks at Class A or Subclass "A" in this period
PRSI Classes other than Class A or Subclass "A" in this period

I certify that the particulars entered above are correct.

Employer   Trade name if different
Address   Date   Phone No.   Fax No.

Revenue On-Line Service   Save Time File P45's on-line using the Revenue On-Line Service.   www.revenue.ie

INSTRUCTIONS TO EMPLOYER
(a) Complete this form when an employee leaves your employment. Take care that all entries are in BLOCK capitals.
(b) Copy PPS Number, Tax Credits, and Standard Rate Cut-Off Point from the latest Certificate of Tax Credits and Standard Rate Cut-Off Point.
(c) If the employee commenced with you after 1st January last include pay and tax notified to you in respect of previous employment. Please insert date of commencement if after the start of this tax year.
(d) Detach Part 1 and send it to your Tax Office immediately. Hand Parts 2, 3 and 4 (unseparated) to the employee when he/she leaves.
(e) If employee has died please send ALL FOUR PARTS of this form (unseparated) to your Tax Office immediately.
(f) A guide to PAYE / PRSI for small employers (IT 50) is available from our Forms & Leaflets Service 1890 306 706 or the Revenue Website.

PART 1

Explanations of Some Items on the Form P45

- - **The Tax Credit and Standard Rate Cut-Off Point** indicates the weekly or monthly amounts for these two items as they were on the date the employee ceased work.
  - The **Month or Week No.** is the month or week number of the income tax year in which the employee ceased work. It is *not* the number of months or weeks that the employee worked with his or her current employer.

- Total Pay and Tax
  - **Part (a)** – if the employee has been employed continuously since 1 January by the same employer, then only item 5(a) must be completed. If the employee started employment since 1 January with the present employer, and if pay and tax since 1 January are known from a previous employer (say from another form P45), then item 5(a) must show the combined totals of pay and tax deducted.
  - **Part (b)** – if the employee started employment any time after 1 January with the present employer, then item 5(b) must be completed.

- - If an employee received a taxable lump sum payment on leaving his or her job, then the amount must be entered here.

- PRSI – This employment only
  - Information under the heading 'PRSI this employment only' refers to the PRSI totals for the present employer and employee only.

Example 5.1

Simon Jones (PPS No.3565879J), Dublin Rd., Athlone, Co. Westmeath was employed by Frank Ryan and Sons Ltd., Mardyke St., Athlone (registered no. 5914368T) from the beginning of the tax year until he left for a new job on 23 June. The details regarding pay, tax, PRSI, etc. are as follows:

- weekly cut-off point €540.00
- weekly tax credit €47.00
- gross pay to date of leaving €12,500.00
- tax paid to date of leaving €1,325.00
- PRSI paid to date of leaving, employee €623.00 and total €1,966.75
- PRSI class – A.

To view the solution, see Figure 5.3.

FIGURE 5.3 FORM P45 FOR SIMON JONES

FORM P45 — CERTIFICATE NO. **U695937** — INCOME TAX - PAY AS YOU EARN - CESSATION CERTIFICATE — **Particulars of Employee Leaving**

PLEASE COMPLETE FORM IN BLOCK CAPITALS

- Surname: JONES
- First Name(s): SIMON
- Unit Number:
- PPS Number: 3565879J
- Date of Leaving: 23 06 0_
- Deceased: (Tick ✔ if applicable)
- Address: DUBLIN RD, ATHLONE, Co. WESTMEATH
- Employer Registered Number: 591438T
- Date of Birth:
- Payroll/Works No.:
- Commencement:

✔ Weekly ◯ Monthly (Please tick ✔ if you are paid weekly or Monthly)

- Weekly/Monthly Tax Credit: 47.00
- Week/Month Number: 25
- Weekly/Monthly Standard Rate Cut-Off Point: 540.00
- Tick ✔ if emergency tax operated:

(a) TOTAL PAY & TAX deducted from 1 January last to date of leaving
- Total Pay: 12,500.00
- Total Tax Deducted: 1,325.00

(b) If Employment commenced since 1 January last enter Pay and Tax deducted for this period of employment only
- Pay: .
- Tax Deducted: .

(c) Amount of Taxable **LUMP SUM PAYMENT** on termination included in either pay figure above - if applicable: 0.00

- (a) Total amount of Taxable Disability Benefit included in Total Pay above: .
- (b) Amount by which Tax Credits were reduced: .
- Amount by which Standard Rate Cut-Off Point was reduced: .
- (c) Indicate that Week 1/Month 1 basis was applied (Tick ✔ if applicable)

Please complete **A, B or C** across where an employee was in receipt of taxable Disability Benefit since 1st January last while employed by you

PRSI - THIS EMPLOYMENT ONLY
- Total PRSI: 1,966.75
- Employee's Share: 623.00
- Total number of weeks of Insurable Employment: 25
- Total number of weeks at Class A or Subclass "A" in this period: 25
- PRSI Classes other than Class A or Subclass "A" in this period:

I certify that the particulars entered above are correct.

- Employer: FRANK RYAN & SONS LTD
- Address: MARDYKE ST, ATHLONE, CO WESTMEATH
- Trade name if different:
- Date: 23 06 0_
- Phone No.:
- Fax No.:

Revenue On-Line Service — Save Time File P45's on-line using the Revenue On-Line Service. — www.revenue.ie

INSTRUCTIONS TO EMPLOYER
(a) Complete this form when an employee leaves your employment. Take care that all entries are in BLOCK capitals.
(b) Copy PPS Number, Tax Credits, and Standard Rate Cut-Off Point from the latest Certificate of Tax Credits and Standard Rate Cut-Off Point.
(c) If the employee commenced with you after 1st January last include pay and tax notified to you in respect of previous employment. Please insert date of commencement if after the start of this tax year.
(d) Detach Part 1 and send it to your Tax Office immediately. Hand Parts 2, 3 and 4 (unseparated) to the employee when he/she leaves.
(e) If employee has died please send ALL FOUR PARTS of this form (unseparated) to your Tax Office immediately.
(f) A guide to PAYE / PRSI for small employers (IT 50) is available from our Forms & Leaflets Service 1890 306 706 or the Revenue Website.

PART 1

QUESTIONS ON COMPLETING FORM P45

Complete a form P45 for each of the following employees, using the form in Appendix G, Figure G.5.

1. Anne Hickey (PPS No. 4450879J), Adelphi Quay, Waterford was employed by Top Class Boutique, Main St, Waterford (registered no. 2241768T) from the beginning of the current tax year until she was dismissed on 26 July. The details regarding pay, tax, PRSI, etc. are as follows:
   - weekly cut-off point €550.00
   - weekly tax credit €45.50
   - gross pay to date of leaving €13,500.00
   - tax paid to date of leaving €1,335.00
   - PRSI paid to date of leaving, employee €657.60 and total €2,277.60
   - PRSI class – A.

2. Michael Fitzgerald (PPS No. 6589752J), Tuam Road, Galway was employed by Horizon Shipping Ltd, Dock Rd, Galway (registered no. 4578632T) from the beginning of the current tax year until he left on 11 April. The details regarding pay, tax, PRSI, etc. are as follows:
   - weekly cut-off point €552.75
   - weekly tax credit €47.82
   - gross pay to date of leaving €9,000.00
   - tax paid to date of leaving €1,270.00
   - PRSI paid to date of leaving, employee €463.80 and total €1,080.00
   - PRSI class – A.

3. Michael Doyle (PPS No. 4452214T), 16 Highfield Rd, Rathgar was employed by IBM from the beginning of the current tax year until he left on 14 March to take up new employment with Compusales (registered no.5412376T), 15 Camden St, Dublin 2. He started on 28 March but left on 29 August to start his own business. The details from both employers are as follows:

	IBM	Compusales
Cumulative gross pay to date of leaving	€6,050.00	€13,800.00
Weekly cut-off point	€562.48	€562.48
Weekly tax credit	€48.20	€48.20
Cumulative tax paid to date of leaving	€506.00	€1,734.00
PRSI paid to date of leaving (employee)	€307.12	€711.16
PRSI paid to date of leaving (total)	€1,033.12	€2,367.16
PRSI class	A	A

DUTIES OF EMPLOYER AT THE END OF THE TAX YEAR

At the end of the income tax year the employer must:

- complete each employee's PAYE and PRSI record for the year just ended
- ensure that a PAYE and PRSI record are set up for each employee for the coming income tax year
- deal with 'week 53' if there is a pay day on 31 December (or in a leap year 30 or 31 December)
- complete and send end-of-year returns to the Revenue Commissioners, P35 Section
- give a form P60 to each employee employed on 31 December.

When Does Week 53 Occur?

'Week 53' occurs when there are fifty-three weekly pay days in the year. This happens when a pay day falls on 31 December or, in a leap year, on 30 or 31 December. The employee is granted one week's tax credit and cut-off point. The employer must operate the 'Week 1' basis for week 53 and calculate tax accordingly. The tax credit and the cut-off point for the next tax year are adjusted to take this into account. See the Income Tax Calendar in Appendix A.

The following are the end-of-year tax forms:

- Form P60
- Form P35

FORM P60 – CERTIFICATE OF PAY, TAX AND PRSI

Between the 31 December and 9 January, the employer must give a form P60 to every employee who was in his or her employment on 31 December. Figure 5.4 shows a form P60.

This form shows the employee's total pay, tax and PRSI contributions for the year ended on 31 December. These figures are taken from the employees' official TDC, 'own system' TDC or computer records. The form must not be given to an employee who was not in the employment on 31 December.

Example 5.2

Brendan Higgins, Racecourse Rd, Naas, Co. Kildare (PPS No. 4587209J) was employed by Tom Jackson & Sons (registered no. 2345862M) for the current tax year. Brendan's gross salary was €28,500. His annual cut-off point was €28,000 and his tax credit was €2,750. He paid class AI PRSI. To view the solution, see Figure 5.4.

Tax Return Forms

FIGURE 5.4 FORM P60 – CERTIFICATE OF PAY, TAX, AND PRSI FOR BRENDAN HIGGINS

P60 PAYE/PRSI

CERTIFICATE OF PAY, TAX AND PAY-RELATED SOCIAL INSURANCE FOR 200_

TO BE GIVEN TO EACH EMPLOYEE WHO WAS IN YOUR EMPLOYMENT ON 31 DECEMBER 200_ WHETHER OR NOT TAX WAS DEDUCTED

NAME: BRENDAN HIGGINS
ADDRESS: RACECOURSE RD., NAAS, CO KILDARE

Personal Public Service No. (PPS No.): 4587209J

If at 31 December 200_
Temporary basis applied enter "1"
Emergency basis applied enter "2"
Week 1/Month 1 basis applied enter "W"

Tax Credit €: 2,750
Standard Rate Cut Off Point €: 28,000
Works Number:
Date of Commencement:
Enter only if date is after 1 Jan 200_:
Employers Unit Code:

If the employee was not in any other employment during the period 1 Jan 200_ to 31 December 200_, the employer need not complete lines 1 and 2 at A and B below. Lines A3 and B3 must always be completed. If an entry is made at line A1 it should equal the sum of the amounts at lines A2 and A3.

PAY

A
1. Total pay in year to 31 December 200_ (including pay in respect of previous employment(s), if any) .... € 28,500
2. Pay in year in respect of previous employment(s), if any, in the year to 31 December 200_ taken into account arriving at the tax deductions made by me/us
3. Pay in respect of THIS employment (i.e. gross pay less superannuation contributions allowable for income tax purposes) .... J6 € 28,500

TAX

B
1. Total net tax deducted in year ended 31 December 200_ (including tax deducted by previous employer(s), if any) .... € 3,060
2. Tax in respect of previous employment(s), if any, in the year to 31 December 200_
3. Net tax deducted in respect of THIS employment .... J7 € 3,060
   OR
   Net tax repaid in respect of THIS employment H9

PRSI IN THIS EMPLOYMENT

C
1. Employee's share of pay-related social insurance contribution .... K3 € 1,445.60
2. Total (i.e. employee's and employer's shares) of pay-related social insurance contribution .... K4 € 4,509.44
3. Total number of weeks of insurable employment inclusive of the number of weeks, if any, at line 6 below F2 52
4. Social insurance contribution class at Dec 200_ or at such later date as employment commenced .... C2 A
5. Second social insurance contribution class/subclass if class changed during this employment .... C3 —
6. Number of weeks of insurable employment at the class entered at line 5 .... F3 —

I/We certify that the particulars given above include the total amount of pay (including overtime, bonus, commission, etc.) paid to you by me/us in the year ended 31 December 200_ the total tax deducted by me/us less any refunds and the total pay-related social insurance contribution in respect of this employment.

P1 Employer's Registered Number: 2345862M
Employer: Tom Jackson & Sons
Date: 10-01-0_

TO THE EMPLOYEE: **THIS IS A VALUABLE DOCUMENT.**

You should retain it carefully as evidence of tax deducted from your income:-

You may also require this document for production to the Collector General if you are claiming repayment of:

(a) PRSI contributions on pay in excess of the pay ceiling for contribution purposes or
(b) the Health Contribution where income was below the relevant threshold for the year.

Form P60 (Rev.)

QUESTIONS ON COMPLETING FORM P60

Use the current rates of tax and PRSI in your calculations (see Appendices C and D).

Complete a P60 for each of the following employees, using the form P60 in Appendix G, Figure G.6.

1. Peter Fitzgerald, 8 Mill Rd, Corbally, Limerick (PPS No.2214534J) was employed by Eason Ltd, Patrick St, Limerick (registered no. 4511732M) since 8 March this tax year. He was paid €380.00 per week. His annual cut-off point was €28,000 and his annual tax credit was €2,350. He paid class A PRSI.
2. Mary O' Sullivan, Tuam Rd, Galway (PPS No.6598074J) was employed by Anthony Ryan's, Shop St, Galway (registered no. 6658732M) since 22 February this tax year. She was paid €450.00 per week. Her annual cut-off point was €29,500 and her annual tax credit was €2,420. She paid class A PRSI.
3. Angela O' Donoghue, 41 Park Drive, Bishopstown, Cork (PPS No.25647879J) was employed by Buckley's Builders' Providers, Wilton, Cork (registered no. 2354009M) since 3 September this tax year. She was paid €680.00 per week. Her annual cut-off point was €28,700 and her annual tax credit was €2,745. She paid class A PRSI. Before joining Buckley's, Anne was employed by John A Wood, Carrigrohane Rd, Cork from the beginning of the tax year. In this job, she was paid €600.00 per week. Her annual cut-off point, tax credit and PRSI details are similar to those with Buckley's Builders.
4. Rashid Khan, 23 Morehampton Rd, Donnybrook, Dublin 4 (PPS No.5689113J) was employed by Lifestyle Sports Ltd, Stillorgan, Co. Dublin (registered no.7845996M) since 2 September this tax year. He was paid €1,280.00 per week. His annual cut-off point was €37,000 and his annual tax credit was €4,440. He paid class A PRSI. Before joining Lifestyle Sports, Rashid was employed by Stillorgan Bowl from the beginning of the tax year. In this job, he was paid €1,200.00 per week. His annual cut-off point, tax credit and PRSI details are similar to those with Lifestyle Sports Ltd.

FORMS P35L AND P35 – EMPLOYER'S ANNUAL RETURN FORMS

At the end of the tax year, the Revenue Commissioners (P35 Section) send the P35 forms to every registered employer.

- Form P35 – the declaration of tax and PRSI for all employees; this is the employer's annual declaration and certificate for tax and PRSI purposes.
- Form P35L – the list of employees and their PPS numbers, on which the employer bases the returns of PAYE and PRSI. If an employee's PPS number is not known, a form P35L/T must be completed. Employers who use a personal computer-based payroll system can return the P35L details on disk. Since April 2001 returns can be made using the Revenue On-Line Service (ROS).

It is important to note the following points:

- a return must be made for every person employed at any time during the tax year even if no tax was deducted
- the data will be transferred directly to computer in the tax office, so it is therefore very important that all entries are written distinctly
- all totals must be rounded to the nearest €; therefore do not use cents
- the particulars on the return form must relate only to employment with the employer; the employer must ensure that the PPS number is exactly as shown on the employee's tax credit certificate and a PPS number must have eight or nine characters (i.e. seven digits and one letter, or seven digits and two letters)
- the closing date for the end-of-year returns to be sent to the Revenue Commissioners, P35 Section, is 15 February.

The Revenue Commissioners place advertisements in the national media to remind employers to send in their returns. There are severe penalties for failure to lodge end-of-year returns within the specified time period.

Example 5.3

The details for the end-of-year return (Form P35L and P35) for Phoenix Enterprises Ltd (registered no. 234567T) are listed in the following table. During the year €26,500 tax and €16,350 PRSI were submitted to the Collector-General.

Employee Name	PPS No.	Total Pay €	Net Tax €	PRSI (EE) Class €	PRSI (Tot) €	Start Date	Finish Date
Carol Ryan	1512887T	18,000	4,240	A1 936	3,096	20 January	
Helen Collins	5687451T	12,500	2,052	A1 579	2,079		18 July
John Kane	1123564M	42,500	10,580	A1 1,759	5,959		
Anne Byrne	3645889J	29,700	9,752	A1 1,697	5,261		

To view the solution, see Figure 5.5 and Figure 5.6.

FIGURE 5.5 FORM P35L

P35L — LIST OF EMPLOYEES WITH PPS NUMBERS IN YEAR ENDED 31ST DECEMBER 200_1_

Name of Employer: PHOENIX ENTERPRISES LTD
Employer's Registration Number: 2345671
GCD: _____ Unit: _____

Personal Public Service Number	Name of Employee	Pay (€)	Net Tax Deducted or Refunded (€)	Employee PRSI (€)	Total PRSI employer & employee (€)	Total Weeks	Initial Class	Other Class	Weeks at Other Class	Finish Date
1512887T	CAROL RYAN	18,000	4240	936	3096	50	A1			
5687451T	HELEN COLLINS	12,500	2052	579	2079	33	A1			18/07/0
1123564M	JOHN KANE	42,500	10580	1759	5959	52	A1			
3645889J	ANNE BYRNE	29,700	9752	1697	5261	52	A1			

PAGE TOTALS: 102700 / 26624 / 4971 / 16395

BBB   See overleaf for guidelines on completion of form.   Remember to subtract net tax refunded i.e. subtract any minus tax amount.

Tax Return Forms

FIGURE 5.6 FORM P35

P35 DECLARATION

RETURN BY 15TH FEBRUARY TO EMPLOYER'S P35 UNIT, NENAGH, CO. TIPPERARY. TEL: 067 33533 X63811.
LO-CALL NUMBER 1890 254565 X63811

AAA

PHOENIX ENTERPRISES LTD

RETURN FOR YEAR ENDED
DAY/MONTH: 31 12 YEAR: 200-

PLEASE QUOTE REGISTRATION NUMBER BELOW IN ALL CORRESPONDENCE.

234567T

SUMMARY OF TAX AND PRSI FOR ALL EMPLOYEES

Please print figures carefully as shown in the boxes provided using a black or blue ball point pen 0 1 2 3 4 5 6 7 8 9

		M5/M6 TOTAL TAX	€ ENTER EURO	TOTAL PRSI S2
A	TOTAL TAX LIABILITY (M5/M6) / TOTAL PRSI LIABILITY (S2)	26624 00		16395 00
B	TOTAL OF ABOVE (TAX + PRSI)		43019 00	
C	TOTAL TAX AND/OR PRSI ALREADY PAID TO THE COLLECTOR-GENERAL		42850 00	
D	BALANCE DUE TO THE COLLECTOR-GENERAL		169 00	
E	OVERPAYMENT FOR WHICH REFUND IS CLAIMED (R1) — IF NO REFUND DUE LEAVE THIS LINE BLANK		0 0	

TO BE SIGNED BY EMPLOYER

I certify and declare that all particulars required to be entered by me in this return are fully and truly stated to the best of my knowledge and belief.

EMPLOYER'S SIGNATURE: *Vincent O'Sullivan*
DATE: 10 - Jan - 200-

CONTACT NAME AND TEL. NO.

FOR OFFICIAL USE ONLY
PAYMENT €.................. SIGN ....

BANK GIRO CREDIT TRANSFER   **PAYSLIP P35**   **Revenue**

To: BANK OF IRELAND
COLLEGE GREEN
DUBLIN 2.

90-71-04

For: COLLECTOR-GENERAL
PAYE/PRSI
A/C. NO. 93288444

NAME: PHOENIX ENTERPRISES LTD   REG. No: 234567T
YEAR ENDED: 31 - 12 - 200-   NOTICE No:

I DECLARE THAT THE AMOUNTS SHOWN BELOW ARE THE BALANCE OF THE AMOUNTS I AM LIABLE TO REMIT TO THE COLLECTOR-GENERAL FOR THE ABOVE YEAR.

SIGNED *Vincent O'Sullivan* DATE 10 - Jan - 200-   DATE REC'D.

	€	c
CASH		00
CHEQUES	169	00
TOTAL	169	00

Receiving Cashiers Brand & Initials

Please do not fold this payslip or write or mark below this line.   Please ensure that this giro accompanies all payments   P.35 EURO

90-71-04 93288444 71

QUESTION ON COMPLETING THE FORMS P35L AND P35

The details for the end-of-year return (forms P35L and P35) for Horizon Ltd (registered no. 5897441T) are listed in the table below. During the current year €22,500 tax and €13,700 PRSI were submitted to the Collector-General.

Employee Name	PPS No.	Total Pay €	Net Tax €	PRSI (EE) Class €	PRSI (Tot) €	Start Date	Finish Date
Ann Flynn	5689114T	8,500	1,092	A1 319	1,339	20 April	
Sean Kelly	4879225T	19,700	4,930	A1 1,047	3,411		5 June
Tom Ryan	5698441M	36,800	12,788	A1 1,645	5,845		
Mary Doyle	7896552J	18,200	3,780	A1 949	3,133		

PART 2

Taxation

Chapter 6

Taxation – Treatment of Married Couples

In this chapter, you will learn about the single and joint assessment methods of taxation for a husband and wife.

Since 1980, tax legislation allows the income of a married woman to be treated separately from that of her husband's. Before 1980, the opposite was the case and the woman's income could not be treated separately from her husband's. Over the years, many changes have been made to the way in which a husband and wife are treated in terms of tax legislation.

YEAR OF MARRIAGE

Once married, a couple should advise the tax office of the date of marriage, quoting each spouse's PPS number. For tax purposes, both partners continue to be treated as two single persons in the year of marriage. However, if the tax paid as two single persons in that year is greater than the tax which would be payable if taxed as a married couple, a refund of the difference can be claimed. Any refund is due only from the date of marriage and will be calculated after the following 31 December.

BASIS OF ASSESSMENT FOR MARRIED COUPLES

A married couple can be assessed in three ways:

- single assessment
- joint assessment
- separate assessment.

SINGLE ASSESSMENT

On this basis, a married couple may want to be assessed as if they were two single individuals. Notice in writing must be given by either spouse to The Inspector of Taxes before the end of the tax year for which the spouse wants to be assessed as a single person. Likewise, notice in writing must be given by the same spouse if the couple want to withdraw from single assessment.

Both spouses:

- are taxed on their own income
- get standard rate cut-off points and tax credits due to a single person
- pay their own tax
- complete their own Return of Income form and claim their credits.

There is *no transferability* of any unused cut-off point or tax credit amounts. Therefore, in most cases this method of assessment for tax is not desirable for tax purposes, as you will see later in this chapter.

JOINT ASSESSMENT

Once a married couple notifies the tax office of their marriage, they are automatically assessed for tax purposes under joint assessment. However, this does not prevent the couple from electing for either single or separate assessment. If either spouse wants to opt out of the joint assessment method, he or she must put the decision in writing.

With joint assessment, a decision has to be made by the couple as to who becomes the *assessable* spouse. The assessable spouse is nominated by both parties jointly. An 'Assessable Spouse Election Form' must be completed and returned to the tax office before the start of the tax year. In the absence of a nomination, the assessable spouse is the spouse with the higher income in the latest year for which details of both spouses' income are known. A spouse will continue to be the assessable spouse unless the couple notifies the tax office to the contrary, in writing.

Under joint assessment, the tax credits can be allocated between the spouses to suit their circumstances. Where the tax office does not receive a request for the allocation of credits, it will normally give all the credits to the assessable spouse, with the exception of the PAYE and employment expenses credits.

SEPARATE ASSESSMENT

This basis of assessment will result in exactly the same total income tax liability as if the couple was jointly assessed. The difference is that each spouse pays his or her own portion of the amount of total tax due, rather than it being a combined total. Effectively the higher income-earning spouse will pay more tax, although this depends on how the tax credits are divided (apportioned) between the couple.

Unlike the single assessment method, any unused credits by one spouse are transferred to the other.

Note: For FETAC assessment purposes, only the single and joint assessment methods are required for examination.

The following examples illustrate the working of the single and joint assessment methods of tax calculation for married couples. The tax rates, bands and credits for a sample tax year are used, as outlined in Chapter 2 (pages 13 to 19).

Example 6.1

Paddy and Mary Clancy, a married couple, have gross salaries of €35,600 and €34,300 respectively.

Single Assessment Method

	Paddy				Mary		
Gross salary	€35,600				€34,300		
	€	€			€	€	
€28,000 x 20% =	5,600			€28,000 x 20% =	5,600		
€7,600 x 42% =	3,192	8,792		€6,300 x 42% =	2,646	8,246	
€35,600				€34,300			

Less credits

	Paddy		Mary	
	€		€	
Personal	1,520		1,520	
PAYE	1,040		1,040	
Total credits		2,560		2,560
Total tax		6,232		5,686

Their total tax liability is €11,918: (€6,232 + €5,686)

Joint Assessment Method

Combined salaries €69,900

	€	€
€56,000 x 20% =	11,200	
€13,900 x 42% =	5,838	17,038
€69,900		

Less credits

	€	
Personal	3,040	
PAYE	2,080	
Total credits		5,120
Total tax		11,918

Example 6.2

Peter and Jane Timmons, a married couple, have gross salaries of €35,500 and €15,200 respectively. They have one incapacitated child (aged six), who is maintained in the proportion 2:1 as to Peter and Jane.

Single Assessment Method

	Peter				Jane		
Gross salary €35,500				€15,200			

	€	€		€	€
€28,000 x 20% =	5,600		€15,200 x 20% =	3,040	
€7,500 x 42% =	3,150	8,750	€ 0 x 42% =	0	3,040
€35,500			€15,200		

Less credits

	€			€	
Personal	1,520			1,520	
PAYE	1,040			1,040	
Incapacitated child	333			167	
Total credits		2,893			2,727
Total tax		5,857			313

Their total tax liability is €6,170: (€5,857 + €313).

Joint Assessment Method

Combined salaries €50,700

	€	€
€50,700 x 20% =	10,140	
€ 0 x 42% =	0	
€50,700		10,140

Less credits

	€	
Personal	3,040	
PAYE	2,080	
Incapacitated child	500	
Total credits		5,620
Total tax		4,520

Note: Using the single assessment method, any used credit is **not transferable**.

In this case the total tax liability is €4,520. The annual tax saving using the joint assessment method is €1,650.

Using the joint assessment method, the combined income amounts to €50,700. This is less than the married couple tax band of €56,000, which means that none of their income is liable for tax at the higher rate.

The reduction in the tax amount is achieved as follows: €7,500 @ 20%, which amounts to €1,500, as opposed to €7,500 @ 42%, which amounts to €3,150; the difference is €1,650.

QUESTIONS ON THE SINGLE AND JOINT ASSESSMENT METHODS

Using the current tax data in your calculations (see Appendix D), calculate the tax liability of the following married couples, employing both the single and joint assessment methods. Note that in some cases you may find that you get the same answer by using both methods. Consider why this might be the case.

1. Niall and Monica Scott have gross salaries of €42,000 and €32,000 respectively.
2. Pat and Aine Dolan have gross salaries of €42,500 and €30,000 respectively.
3. David and Mary Kennedy have gross salaries of €20,000 and €40,000 respectively. David's aged mother lives with the family.
4. Tom and Rita Smith have gross salaries of €20,000 and €35,200 respectively. Their incapacitated child is maintained in the proportion 1:2 as to Tom and Rita.

Chapter 7

Annual Take-Home Salary and Budgetary Changes

In this chapter, you will learn:

- how to calculate an individual's annual take-home salary from given data
- how to assess the effect of budgetary changes on an individual's annual take-home salary.

CALCULATING TAKE-HOME SALARY

Use the current rates of tax and PRSI (see Appendices C and D). You can use the following format to calculate the take-home salary, where x indicates a number.

Format

		€	€	€	€
1	**GROSS SALARY**		xx,xxx		
2	Less superannuation / health benefit		x,xx		
3	Reckonable earnings (line 1-2)				xx,xxx
4	**TAX**				
5	€ Cut-off point (band) @ %	x,xxx			
6	€ Balance @ %	x,xxx			
7	Total (line 5+6)		x,xxx		
8					
9	*Less credits*				
10	Personal	x,xxx			
11	PAYE	x,xxx			
12	Incapacitated child	x,xxx			
13	Dependent relative	x,xxx			
14	Total credits (lines 10 to 14)		x,xxx		
15	*Total tax due (line 7-15)*			x,xxx	

Annual Take-Home Salary and Budgetary Changes

		€	€	€	€
16	**PRSI**				
17	PRSI @ class				
18	€x,xxx @ %		x,xxx		
19	€x,xxx @ %		x,xxx		
20	Total PRSI (line 18+19)			xxxx	
21	Total deductions (line 15+20)				xx,xxx
22	**TAKE-HOME PAY (line 3-21)**				xx,xxx

Example 7.1

Lynda O'Toole, a single person, earns €35,000 gross salary. She pays a total of 5% towards pension and salary protection. Her annual cut-off point is €28,000 and she is entitled to the basic tax credits. She pays class A1 PRSI.

Solution

		€	€	€	€
1	**GROSS SALARY**		35,000		
2	Less superannuation / health benefit		1,750		
3	Reckonable earnings (line 1-2)				33,250
4	**TAX**				
5	€28,000 @ 20%	5,600			
6	€ 5,250 @ 42%	2,205			
7	Total (line 5+6)		7,805		
8					
9	*Less credits*				
10	Personal	1,520			
11	PAYE	1,040			
12	Incapacitated child	0,000			
13	Dependent relative	0,000			
14	Total credits (lines 10 to13)		2,560		
15	Total tax due (line 7-14)			5,245	
16	**PRSI**				
17	€6,604 @ 2.0%		132		
18	€26,646 @ 6.0%		1,599		
19	Total PRSI (line 17+18)			1,731	
20	Total deductions (line 15+19)				6,976
21	**TAKE-HOME PAY (line 3-20)**				26,274

Example 7.2

Tim and Catherine Buckley, a married couple, earn €36,000 and €30,000 gross salaries respectively. They are jointly assessed for tax and Tim has elected to be the assessable spouse. They both pay 5% towards pension. Their annual cut-off point is €56,000. They are entitled to the basic tax credits. They both pay class A1 PRSI.

Solution

		€	€	€	€
1	**GROSS SALARY**		66,000		
2	Less superannuation / health benefit		3,300		
3	Reckonable earnings (line 1-2)				62,700
4	**TAX**				
5	€56,000 @ 20 %	11,200			
6	€ 6,700 @ 42 %	2,814			
7	Total (line 5+6)		14,014		
8					
9	*Less credits*				
10	Personal	3,040			
11	PAYE	2,080			
12	Incapacitated child	0,000			
13	Dependent relative	0,000			
14	Total credits (lines 10 to 13)		5,120		
15	Total tax due (line 7-14)			8,894	
16	**PRSI**				
17	€13,208 @ 2.0%		264		
18	€49,492 @ 6.0%		2,970		
19	Total PRSI (line 17+18)			3,234	
20	Total deductions (line 15+19)				12,128
21	**TAKE-HOME PAY (line 3-21)**				50,572

QUESTIONS ON CALCULATING TAKE-HOME PAY

Use the relevant current tax and PRSI data in your calculations (see Appendices C and D).

Calculate the annual take-home pay for the following employees.

1. Anne Costello, a single person, earning a gross salary of €22,000. Her annual cut-off point is equivalent to the fixed tax band and she qualifies for the basic tax credits. She pays class D1 PRSI.
2. David Fitzgerald, a single person, earning a gross salary of €34,000. He pays 5% towards pension. His annual cut-off point is equivalent to the fixed tax band and he qualifies for the basic tax credits. He pays class A1 PRSI.
3. Tom Kelly, a married person, earning a gross salary of €46,000. His wife does not work outside the home. He pays 5% towards pension. His annual cut-off point is

equivalent to the fixed tax band and he qualifies for the basic tax credits. He pays class A1 PRSI.

4. Liam and Jane Higgins, a married couple, earn €34,000 and €37,000 respectively. They are jointly assessed for tax and Jane has elected to be the assessable spouse. The annual cut-off point is equivalent to the fixed tax band. They qualify for the basic tax credits. Liam's elderly mother lives with the family and is maintained by them. They have a seven-year-old child with special needs. They pay class A1 PRSI.

EFFECT OF BUDGETARY CHANGES ON TAKE-HOME PAY

In October of each year, the Minister for Finance announces details of the Government's forthcoming financial budget for the country. The budget is discussed and finally passed into legislation through the Finance Act in November.

For most people the main items of interest in the budget announcements are the changes in tax rates, tax credits, tax bands and social welfare payments. Changes in customs and excise duties usually have immediate effect. That is why the prices of drink, tobacco and petrol usually increase at midnight on budget day! Changes in social welfare payments usually come into effect later in the year. All changes relating to personal taxation (tax, PRSI, etc.) come into effect on 1 January, which is the start of the new tax year.

Example 7.3 on page 86 shows how changes in the budget affect take-home pay. Two sample tax years are used for comparison purposes.

The relevant details for both years are as follows:

	Year 1	Year 2
TAX RATES		
Standard tax rate	22%	20%
Higher tax rate	44%	42%
TAX BANDS		
Single tax band	€26,000	€28,000
Married tax band*	€52,000	€56,000
TAX CREDITS		
Single personal credit	€1,400	€1,550
Married personal credit	€2,800	€3,100
PAYE credit	€ 700	€ 800
Dependent relative (max)	€ 60	€ 70
Incapacitated child (max)	€ 400	€ 500
PRSI RATES		
PRSI class A1 ceiling	€38,000	€40,500
First € 6,604	2.0%	2.0%
Next €31,396	6.0%	N/A
Next €33,896	N/A	6.0%
Balance	2.0%	2.0%

* **Note:** Assume both spouses are working and their earnings exceed band thresholds.

Example 7.3

Paul and Siobhan Dolan, a married couple, earn €35,000 each. They are jointly assessed for tax and Paul has elected to be the assessable spouse. They both pay class A1 PRSI.

Solution

		€	€	€	€
		Year 1		Year 2	
1	**GROSS SALARY**	70,000		70,000	
2	Less superannuation / health benefit	000		000	
3	Reckonable earnings (line 1-2)	70,000		70,000	
4	**TAX**				
5	€52,000 @ 22%	11,440			
6	€18,000 @ 44%	7,920			
7	Total (line 5+6)		19,360		
8	**TAX**				
9	€56,000 @ 20 %			11,200	
10	€14,000 @ 42 %			5,880	
11	Total (line 9+10)				17,080
12					
13	*Less credits*				
14	Personal	2,800		3,100	
15	PAYE	1,400		1,600	
16	Total credits (line 14+15)		4,200		4,700
17	Total tax due (line 7 or 11 – 16)		15,160		12,380
18	**PRSI**				
19	€13,208 @ 2.0%	264			
20	€56,792 @ 6.0%	3,408			
22	Total PRSI (lines 19+20)		3,672		
22	**PRSI**				
23	€13,208 @ 2.0%			264	
24	€56,792 @ 6.0%			3,408	
25	Total PRSI (line 23+24)				3,672
26	Total deductions (line 17+(21 or 25))		18,832		16,052
27	**TAKE-HOME PAY(line 3-26)**		51,168		53,948

The difference in take-home pay between the two years is €2,780.

QUESTIONS ON CALCULATING TAKE-HOME PAY IN DIFFERENT YEARS

Compare the take-home pay for two tax years for the following employees. You can compare the current tax year with that of next year or any other combinations you choose (see Appendix E).

1. Mick Byrne, a single person, earning a gross salary of €20,000. He pays class B1 PRSI.
2. Deirdre Cairns, a single person, earning a gross salary of €35,000. She pays class A1 PRSI.
3. Tom Higgins, a single person, earning a gross salary of €50,000. He pays class A1 PRSI.
4. Frank and Anne Walsh, a married couple, earning €34,000 and €37,500 respectively. They pay class D1 PRSI.
5. Mark and Siobhan Reid, a married couple, earning a gross salary of €58,000. Siobhan does not work outside the home. Mark's mother, who is infirm, lives with the family and is maintained by them. He pays class D1 PRSI.

PART 3

Computer Payroll

Chapter 8

Computer Payroll

This chapter contains the following sections:
- advantages of a computerised payroll system
- sample examination paper.

In years past, most businesses and organisations in the country did not have a computerised payroll system. This was largely due to two factors:
- software and trained staff were not available
- buying software and training staff were too expensive.

Today most, if not all, businesses and organisations have computerised their payroll systems. A number of businesses, however (particularly those with a large workforce), sub-contract their payroll to an agency or bureau. The Revenue Commissioners are encouraging employers to computerise their records, and are giving them as much assistance as possible. The online service (ROS) was set up to achieve this aim. A number of off-the-shelf payroll packages are available at competitive prices at present, which is encouraging for employers.

ADVANTAGES OF A COMPUTERISED PAYROLL SYSTEM

The advantages of a computerised payroll system over a manual one include the following:
- speed – information is processed much faster using a computerised system
- accuracy – it is rare that mistakes are made using a computerised payroll system unless the operator incorrectly enters the information to be processed
- user-friendliness – most packages are easy to learn and operate; however, success depends on the user's knowledge of how the PAYE system works in the manual format
- reporting – computerised payroll packages enable users to produce reports such as departmental analysis, gross to net figures, employee payment history, cash analysis and timekeeping and attendance reports, which are useful for managerial staff in any organisation or business
- confidentiality – senior management can allow or deny access to some or all of the information of an organisation's employee records (using password protection), thus ensuring privacy

- end-of-term returns – computerised payroll systems enable companies to produce reports and certificates such as the P30s (CC124), P45s, P60s and the P35 in a matter of seconds, compared to hours perhaps for a manual system.

> **Note**
>
> Because of the variety of different packages that are available, instructions on how to operate a computer payroll package are not given in this book. Furthermore, the FETAC computer payroll examination is not package specific, thus enabling the teacher / trainer to devise his or her own examination paper based on the guidelines provided (see Module Descriptor).

Teachers must ensure that all the assessment criteria are addressed for assessment purposes. For more information, see the Module Descriptor.

The following sample exercise and examination papers should be suitable for all computer payroll packages. You can modify some of the details to suit the particular requirements of your package.

SAMPLE EXERCISE ON A COMPUTERISED PAYROLL SYSTEM

You are required to do the following.

1. Set up the following two employees on the payroll system from the data supplied.
2. Set up the payments (i.e. bonus etc.) and deductions (i.e. VHI etc.) for the company.
3. Process the payroll for the first week of the tax year on 5 January.
4. Save the data (timesheets) for this period.
5. Set up the next pay period.
6. Edit employee data, as necessary. This may include changes in tax credits, voluntary deductions, etc.
7. Process the payroll for the second week on 12 January.
8. Save the data (timesheets) for this period.
9. Make a back-up of your data on floppy disk.
10. Print the following reports for the two employees on 12 January:
    (i) pay slips
    (ii) a Gross to Net report
    (iii) an 'Employee Details' report
    (iv) a 'Departmental Analysis' report
    (v) a CC124 (P30) report.

Note to teacher / trainer: Insert the appropriate data in the blank spaces provided.

Computer Payroll

INPUT DETAILS

	Employee No.1	Employee No.2
Name	Michael Ryan	Tariq Yousufi,
Address	'Somerton', Moycullen Co. Galway	Cathedral Ave, Tuam, Co. Galway
Marital status	Single	Married
D.O.B.	12-08-1968	14-06-1972
Start date with company	03-05-1994	10-09-1997
Department	Accounts	Administration
PPS No.	5282041K	3492426L
Tax status	Normal	Normal
Annual cut-off point	€	€
Weekly cut-off point	€	€
Annual tax credit	€	€
Weekly tax credit	€	€
PRSI class	A	A
PRSI base code (highest)	A1	A1
Basic salary	N/A	€850.00
Standard hours	39	N/A
Rate per hour	€12.50	N/A
Payment method	Cheque	Cheque
	WEEKLY DEDUCTIONS:	
Pension/PRSA %	N/A	3%
Trade union	€ 5.75	€ 5.75
VHI	€ 9.50	€12.75
Social club	€ 4.00	€ 4.00
	TIMESHEET ENTRIES FOR WEEK NO.1	
	Michael Ryan	**Tariq Yousufi**
	Payments	**Payments**
	2 hours time and half 3 hours double time Bonus €35.00	Commission €80.00
	TIMESHEET ENTRIES FOR WEEK NO.2	
	Payments	**Payments**
	3 hours time and half 5 hours double time Bonus €40.00	Commission €40.00 Expenses €85.68

SAMPLE EXAMINATION PAPER 1

Instructions to candidates

You work in the Accounts Department of Sloan & Co. Ltd with responsibility for the company's payroll. A new computer payroll system has just been installed and you are required to transfer the data for the company's employees onto this new system.

Carry out the following tasks.

1. Set up the following four employees on the payroll system from the data supplied on pages 95 to 96.
2. Set up the payments and deductions for the company.
3. Set the pay period for the company for week 51 on 19 December.
4. Process the payroll for week 51 for all the employees, from the timesheet data.
5. Save the data (timesheets) for this period.
6. Set the next pay period for week 52 on 26 December.
7. Edit the employee's data, as necessary.
8. Process the payroll again for week 52 from the timesheet data.
9. Save the data (timesheets) for this period.
10. Make a back-up of your data on floppy disk.
11. Print the following reports on 26 December for all employees:
    (i) pay slips
    (ii) a Gross to Net report
    (iii) an 'Employee Details' report
    (iv) a CC124 (P30) report.
    (v) a P60 for the first two employees.
12. Hand your signed printouts and disk to the Invigilator.

Computer Payroll

INPUT DETAILS

	Employee No.1	**Employee No.2**
Name	Frank Smith	Sheila Ryan
Address	Gorey	Gorey
	Co. Wexford	Co. Wexford
D.O.B.	12-06-1967	14-03-1971
Marital status	Single	Married
Start date with company	03-04-1995	10-02-1992
Department	HR	Administration
PPS No.	5282041K	3492426L
Tax status	Normal	Normal
Annual cut-off point	€	€
Weekly cut-off point	€	€
Annual tax credit	€	€
Weekly tax credit	€	€
Basic salary	N/A	€
Standard hours	39	N/A
Rate per hour	€9.80	N/A
Payment method	Cheque	Cheque
PRSI class	A	A
PRSI base code (highest)	A1	A1
Gross pay YTD	€	€
Pension paid YTD	€	€
Tax paid YTD	€	€
Net pay YTD	€	€
PRSI (EE) paid YTD	€	€
PRSI (ER) paid YTD	€	€
PRSI (Tot) paid YTD	€	€
	WEEKLY DEDUCTIONS:	
Pension/PRSA %	N/A	3%
Trade union	€ 4.00	€ 4.00
VHI	€ 9.50	€11.75
Social club	€ 5.00	€ 5.00
	TIMESHEET ENTRIES FOR WEEK NO.51	
	Frank Smith	**Sheila Ryan**
	Payments	**Payments**
	2 hours time and half	Commission €80.00
	4 hours double time	
	Bonus €42.00	
	TIMESHEET ENTRIES FOR WEEK NO.52	
	Payments	**Payments**
	3 hours time and half	Commission €58.00
	5 hours double time	Expenses €75.60
	Bonus €25.75	

EMPLOYEE DETAILS

	Employee No.3	**Employee No.4**
Name	Jean Cloney	Helen Dixon
Address	Main St, Bray	Church St, Bunclody
	Co. Wicklow	Co. Wexford
D.O.B.	12-08-1972	14-06-1967
Marital status	Single	Married
Start date with company	12 Dec (this year)	10 Nov (this year)
Department	Accounts	Marketing
PPS No.	4352041K	2642426L
Tax status	Emergency	Week 1/ Month 1
Annual cut-off point	N/A	€
Weekly cut-off point	N/A	€
Annual tax credit	N/A	€
Weekly tax credit	€	€
Basic salary	N/A	€
Standard hours	39	N/A
Rate per hour	€10.00	N/A
Payment method	Cheque	Cheque
PRSI class	A	A
PRSI base code (highest)	A1	A1
Gross pay YTD	Nil	€
Pension paid YTD	Nil	€
Tax paid YTD	Nil	€
Net pay YTD	Nil	€
PRSI (EE) paid YTD	Nil	€
PRSI (ER) paid YTD	Nil	€
PRSI (Tot) paid YTD	Nil	€
	WEEKLY DEDUCTIONS:	
Pension amount and %	N/A	3%
Trade union	€ 2.50	€ 4.00
VHI	€ 0.00	€ 8.75
Social club	€ 0.00	€ 5.00
	TIMESHEET ENTRIES FOR WEEK NO.51	
	Jean Cloney	**Helen Dixon**
	Payments	**Payments**
	3 hours time and half	Commission €22.80
	5 hours double time	
	TIMESHEET ENTRIES FOR WEEK NO.52	
	Payments	**Payments**
	5 hours time and half	Commission €43.25
	7 hours double time	Expenses €45.65
	Bonus €25.75	

Computer Payroll 97

> **Note:**
> Insert the current data in the blank spaces provided for tax and PRSI figures.

SAMPLE EXAMINATION PAPER 2

Instructions to candidates

You work in the Accounts Department of Sloan & Co. Ltd. with responsibility for the company's payroll. A new computer payroll system has just been installed and you are required to transfer the data for the company's employees onto this new system.

Carry out the following tasks.

1. Set up the following four employees on the payroll system from the data supplied on pages 98 to 99.
2. Set up the payments and deductions for the company.
3. Set the pay period for the company for week 51 on 19 December.
4. Process the payroll for week 51 for all the employees, from the timesheet data.
5. Save the data (timesheets) for this period.
6. Set the next pay period for week 52 on 26 December.
7. Edit the employee's data, as necessary.
8. Process the payroll again for week 52 from the timesheet data.
9. Save the data (timesheets) for this period.
10. Make a back-up of your data on floppy disk.
11. Print the following reports on 26 December for all employees:
    (i) pay slips
    (ii) a Gross to Net report
    (iii) an 'Employee Details' report
    (iv) a CC124 report (P30).
12. Hand your signed printouts and disk to the Invigilator.

INPUT DETAILS

	Employee No.1	**Employee No.2**
Name	Frank Smith	Sheila Ryan
Address	Gorey	Gorey
	Co. Wexford	Co. Wexford
D.O.B.	12-06-1967	14-03-1971
Marital status	Single	Married
Start date with company	03-04-1990	10-02-1992
Department	HR	Administration
PPS No.	5282041K	3492426L
Tax status	Normal	Normal
Annual cut-off point	€	€
Weekly cut-off point	€	€
Annual tax credit	€	€
Weekly tax credit	€	€
Basic salary	N/A	€800.00
Standard hours	39	N/A
Rate per hour	€9.80	N/A
Payment method	Cheque	Cheque
PRSI class	A	A
PRSI base code (highest)	A1	A1
Gross pay YTD	€20,000.00	€40,000.00
Pension paid YTD	€ 0.00	€ 2,000.00
Tax paid YTD	€	€
Net pay YTD	€	€
PRSI (EE) paid YTD	€	€
PRSI (ER) paid YTD	€	€
PRSI (Tot) paid YTD	€	€
	WEEKLY DEDUCTIONS:	
Pension amount and %	N/A	5%
Trade union	€ 4.00	€ 4.00
VHI	€11.50	€12.50
Social club	€ 5.00	€10.00
	TIMESHEET ENTRIES FOR WEEK NO.51	
	Frank Smith	**Sheila Ryan**
	Payments	**Payments**
	2 hours time and half	Commission €80.00
	4 hours double time	
	Bonus €42.00	
	TIMESHEET ENTRIES FOR WEEK NO.52	
	Payments	**Payments**
	3 hours time and half	Commission €58.00
	5 hours double time	Expenses €75.60
	Bonus €25.75	

Computer Payroll

INPUT DETAILS

	Employee No.3	**Employee No.4**
Name	Jean Cloney	Helen Dixon
Address	Main St, Bray	Church St, Bunclody
	Co. Wicklow	Co. Wexford
D.O.B.	12-08-1972	14-06-1967
Marital status	Single	Married
Start date with company	12 Dec (this year)	10 Nov (this year)
Department	Accounts	Marketing
PPS No.	5282041K	2642426L
Tax status	Emergency	Week 1/ Month 1
Annual cut-off point	N/A	€
Weekly cut-off point	N/A	€
Annual tax credit	N/A	€
Weekly tax credit	€	€
Basic salary	N/A	€675.00
Standard hours	39	N/A
Rate per hour	€10.00	N/A
Payment method	Cheque	Cheque
PRSI class	A	A1
PRSI base code (highest)	A1	A1
Gross pay YTD	Nil	€
Pension paid YTD	Nil	€
Tax paid YTD	Nil	€
Net pay YTD	Nil	€
PRSI (EE) paid YTD	Nil	€
PRSI (ER) paid YTD	Nil	€
PRSI (Tot) paid YTD	Nil	€
	Weekly deductions:	
Pension amount and %	N/A	3%
Trade union	€ 0.00	€ 4.00
VHI	€ 9.80	€15.00
Social club	€ 5.00	€10.00
	TIMESHEET ENTRIES FOR WEEK NO.51	
	Jean Cloney	**Helen Dixon**
	Payments	**Payments**
	3 hours time and half	Commission €22.80
	5 hours double time	
	TIMESHEET ENTRIES FOR WEEK NO.52	
	Payments	**Payments**
	5 hours time and half	Commission €43.25
	7 hours double time	Expenses €45.65
	Bonus €25.75	

PART 4

Revision

Chapter 9

Revision Assignments

This chapter contains the following sections.

- Quiz
- Revision Assignment 1
- Revision Assignment 2
- Sample FETAC examination paper and project brief.

In this chapter, you will have the opportunity to test your knowledge and skills on all aspects of the *Payroll—Manual and Computerised* course. Let's start with a quiz!

QUIZ

Answer the following questions. To indicate your answer, circle the letter *T* or *F*.

If you score full marks, it will have been an excellent year's work.

1. Net pay is take-home pay. (T or F)
2. Overtime is not taxed. (T or F)
3. There are only fifty-two weeks in the tax year. (T or F)
4. It is the employer's responsibility to get a tax credit certificate for his or her employee(s). (T or F)
5. An employer can have two PAYE registration numbers. (T or F)
6. The Home Carer's tax credit is available to married couples who are taxed as single persons. (T or F)
7. ROS is the Revenue online service. (T or F)
8. Tax relief for medical insurance is given at source. (T or F)
9. PRSA means Private Retirement Savings Allowance. (T or F)
10. The standard rate cut-off point is always equivalent to the tax band. (T or F)
11. Tax bands are individualised for married couples. (T or F)
12. Individuals over the age of fifty-five are exempt from PRSI. (T or F)
13. There is no income ceiling on the employer's PRSI contribution. (T or F)
14. People within class A PRSI include those public servants that were employed from 6 April 1995. (T or F)
15. TDC means Tax Deduction Category. (T or F)
16. If the cumulative cut-off point exceeds the cumulative gross pay in a particular week, tax is calculated on the cumulative gross pay only. (T or F)

17. The cut-off point for the first four weeks of employment on the emergency system is always €500 per week. (T or F)
18. Part 1 of the form P45 is sent directly to the Inspector of Taxes by the employer, for an employee ceasing work. (T or F)
19. The form P60 is sent by the employer to the Inspector of Taxes at the end of the tax year. (T or F)
20. Married couples who opt for single assessment for tax purposes always pay more tax than if they had opted for joint assessment. (T or F)

The answers are on page 117.

REVISION ASSIGNMENT 1

Note: These questions review the material in Chapters 1 to 4. Use the relevant information on tax and PRSI for the current tax year in your calculations (see Appendices C and D).

Answer the following questions.

1. Calculate the gross pay for John Higgins from the following details:
   - standard pay €341.25 for a thirty-nine hour week
   - overtime worked – Monday, two hours – Wednesday, three hours – Friday, one hour – Saturday, three hours.

Use the overtime rates in Chapter 1 on page 6.

2. Calculate the annual tax credit for the current year for the following two employees.
   - Ita Greene is single.
   - John and Rita Finlay, a married couple, are jointly assessed for tax. John is the assessable spouse. John's aged mother lives with the family and is supported by them.

3. Complete the cumulative TDC for Michael Shaughnessy, a single person, for the first eight weeks of the tax year from the following details:
   - his standard pay is €600.00 (weekly) for a forty-hour week
   - the first pay day is 5 January
   - he does overtime worth €75.00 and €86.00 in weeks two and four respectively
   - he takes a week's holiday (annual leave) in week seven
   - he pays 5% into a PRSA
   - he is entitled to the basic tax credits and standard rate tax band (cut-off point)
   - he pays class A PRSI
   - amounts of €15.00 and €7.50 are deducted from his pay each week for the credit union and canteen expenses respectively.

4. Complete the cumulative TDC for Kathrina Mooney, a married person, for five weeks starting from 8 January from the following details:
   - her standard pay is €420.00 per week
   - she receives a benefit-in-kind valued at €32.00 per week
   - she took a week's unpaid leave in her third week of work
   - she is entitled to the basic tax credits and standard rate tax band (cut-off point) and these are divided equally between herself and her husband
   - she pays class A PRSI
   - amounts of €10.00 and €8.55 are deducted from her pay each week for trade union subscription and canteen expenses respectively.

5. Kate O'Toole, a single person, started work and her first pay day was on 8 February. She spent nine weeks on emergency tax. The following week she was transferred to the cumulative tax system. Complete her emergency TDC for the nine weeks and the first two weeks of her cumulative TDC. The details are as follows:
   - she earns €380.00 per week
   - she pays class B PRSI
   - she is entitled to the basic tax credits and standard rate tax band (cut-off point) when she transfers to cumulative tax.

6. Frank Dillon, a married person, started work in March and his first pay day was 10 March. He was placed on temporary tax for three weeks, earning €475.00 per week. He is entitled to the basic tax credits and standard rate tax band, shared equally with his wife. He pays class D PRSI. Complete his temporary TDC for the first three weeks and the cumulative TDC for the first two weeks after he was transferred to this system.

REVISION ASSIGNMENT 2

Note: These questions review the material in Chapters 5 to 7. Use the relevant information on tax and PRSI for the current tax year in your calculations (see Appendices C and D).

Answer the following questions.

1. Write an explanatory note on the form P30.

2. Prepare a P45 from the following details.
   Roger Hynes (PPS No.2356789M), 23 Sandymount Drive, Ballsbridge, Dublin 4 was employed by RTE from the beginning of the tax year until he left on 3 June. He took up new employment with Higgins & Associates (registered no. 3426761T), 6 Main St, Dun Laoghaire. He started his new job on 11 June but he left to take a career break on 28 September. The details from both employers follow.

Employer	Cum Gross Pay (weekly)	Cum Cut-Off Point	Cum Tax Credit	Cum Tax Paid	PRSI - A1 (EE)	PRSI - AI (Tot)
RTE	€11,000	€11,858	€990	€1,022.32	€548.27	€1,730.77
Higgins & Ass.	€19,400	€21,021	€1,755	€2,033.72	€827.82	€2,913.32

3. Prepare a P60 from the following details.
   Maura Mee, Bundoran, Co. Donegal (PPS No.2398772J) was employed by Donegal Co-Op, Main St, Donegal (registered no. 3487665T) for the current tax year. Her salary was €32,800. She is a married person and she shares her basic tax credits and cut-off point equally with her husband. Her mother lives with the family and is maintained by them. She paid class A1 PRSI.

4. Complete the P35L and the P35 for the current year for Best West Café Ltd (registered no. 2345710K) from the data below.

Employee Name	PPS No.	Total Pay €	Net Tax €	PRSI (EE) Class	€	PRSI (Tot) €	Start date	Finish date
Anne Doyle	2514778N	19,000	4,785	A1	1,001	3,044		4 July
Tom Hanks	6832114P	24,500	6,210	A1	1,359	3,993	6 April	
Frank Wall	9987441K	21,000	5,824	A1	1,131	3,389		
Jane Gordon	6512447T	32,000	10,580	A1	1,549	4,989		

During the year Best West Café submitted €27,200 tax and €15,400 PRSI to the Collector-General.

5. Calculate the tax liability of the following married couple, using both single and joint assessment methods.
   Michael and Mary have gross salaries of €24,000 and €32,500 respectively. Mary is the assessable spouse. Michael's aged mother lives with the family and is maintained by them.

6. Assess the effect of the budget on the take-home pay of a married couple who are jointly assessed for tax. Their combined salary is €60,000. They are entitled to the basic tax credits and standard rate tax band. They both pay class AI PRSI. You may use any two tax years for comparison purposes.

SAMPLE FETAC EXAMINATION PAPER

COMPUTER PAYROLL EXAMINATION

Date: May 200_
Time Allowed: 2 hours (excluding printing time)

INSTRUCTIONS TO CANDIDATES

You are employed in the wages section of Phoenix Ltd and your job is to look after payroll. You are required to transfer the firm's staff onto the computerised system, which has just been installed.

The following tasks have to be carried out:

1. Enter the appropriate 'Payments' and 'Deductions' in the Company Set Up.
2. Enter the five employees from the details supplied on pages 108 to 112.

Note: Add your initials to the surname of *each* employee for identification purposes.

3. Set the first Pay Period to 19 December 200_ (i.e. week 51).
4. Process the payroll for the five employees on this date from the data supplied.
5. Set the next Pay Period to 26 December 200_ (i.e. week 52).
6. Edit the data for any of the employees where appropriate.
7. Process the payroll again for the first four employees in week 52.
8. Make a backup of your data on floppy disk.
9. Print the following reports on 26 December, 200_
   (i) an 'Employee Details Report' for **each** employee
   (ii) a 'Gross to Net' Report
   (iii) a CC124 report (P30)
   (iv) a P45 for Teresa Kelly
   (v) payslips for **each** employee.
   (vi) a P60 for the first two employees.
10. **Sign** your printouts and hand them together with your disk to the invigilator.

EMPLOYEE PROFILE

Employee No. 1	
Name:	Brendan Ryan
Address:	18 Merrion Rd, Ballsbridge, Dublin 4
PPS No.	3565771J
Cost Code:	Accounts
Pay method:	Cheque
Gross salary (weekly):	€530.50
Tax status:	Normal
Tax credit:	€45.50
Cut-off point:	€542.46
PRSI Class:	A
Insurable weeks:	50
Start date with the company:	21-06-1998
Gross earnings (less pension) YTD:	€25,729.00
Tax paid YTD:	€3,021.00
Net earnings YTD:	€16,509.50
PRSI paid YTD:	EE = €1,290.50
PRSI paid YTD:	ER = €3,087.50
Pension paid YTD:	EE = €796.00

Timesheet entries

	Payment	Deductions
Week 51	Commission €30.65 Bonus €32.89	Pension €15.92 Trade Union €8.63 VHI €22.75

Additional information:

Brendan's tax credit increased to €47.00 effective in week 52.

Timesheet entries

	Payments	Deductions
Week 52	Commission €58.50 Expenses €55.69	Pension €15.92 Trade Union €8.63 VHI €22.75

EMPLOYEE PROFILE

Employee No. 2	
Name:	Helen Keogh
Address:	25 Cedarwood Rd, Glasnevin, Dublin 11
PPS No.	2881428B
Cost Code:	HR
Pay method:	Cheque
Gross salary (weekly):	€562.85
Tax status:	Normal
Tax credit:	€45.65
Cut-off point:	€542.31
PRSI Class:	A
Insurable weeks:	50
Start date with the company:	23-03-1994
Gross earnings (less pension) YTD:	€26,735.50
Tax paid YTD:	€3,222.00
Net earnings YTD:	€20,059.50
PRSI paid YTD:	EE = €1,350.00
PRSI paid YTD:	ER = €3,208.50
Pension paid YTD:	EE = €1,407.00

Note: Helen took out a company loan of €600.00 recently. She is to pay back €30.00 weekly until the loan is cleared.

Timesheet entries

	Payment	Deductions
Week 51	Commission €75.65	Pension €28.14 Trade Union €8.63 VHI €33.45 and Loan

Timesheet entries

	Payments	Deductions
Week 52	Commission €100.00 Expenses €40.00	Pension €28.14 Trade Union €8.63 VHI €33.45 and Loan

EMPLOYEE PROFILE

Employee No. 3	
Name:	Robert Moore
Address:	26 Waterloo Rd, Ballsbridge, Dublin 4
PPS No.	1285988J
Cost Code:	Administration
Pay method:	Cheque
Hourly rate:	€7.20
Standard hours:	39
Tax status:	Emergency
PRSI Class:	A
Insurable weeks:	Nil
Start date with the company:	12 December this year
Gross earnings (less pension) YTD:	Nil
Tax paid YTD:	Nil
Net earnings YTD:	Nil
PRSI paid YTD:	Nil
Pension paid YTD:	Nil

Timesheet entries

	Payment	Deductions
Week 51	5 hours time and half 3 hours double time	Trade Union €8.63

Additional information:
Robert joined the company social club on 22 December paying €5.00 per week

Timesheet entries

	Payments	Deductions
Week 52	3 hours time and half Bonus €16.50	Trade Union €8.63

EMPLOYEE PROFILE

Employee No. 4	
Name:	Fiona Shaw
Address:	6 The Maples, Greenlea Dr., Terenure, Dublin 6
PPS No:	5282041K
Cost Code:	Marketing
Pay method:	Cheque
Hourly rate:	€12.00
Standard hours:	39
Tax status:	Week1/ Month 1
Tax credit:	€46.40
Cut-off point:	€542.25
PRSI Class:	A
Insurable weeks:	50
Start date with the company:	15 December this year
Gross earnings (less pension) with previous employer:	€14,040.00
Tax paid with previous employer:	€1,416.00
Net earnings YTD:	€11,292.60
PRSI paid YTD:	EE = €690.00
PRSI paid YTD:	ER = €1,684.80
Pension paid YTD:	Nil

Timesheet entries

	Payment	Deductions
Week 51	6 hours time and half 4 hours double time	Trade Union €8.63 VHI €12.75

Timesheet entries

	Payments	Deductions
Week 52	4 hours time and half 3 hours double time	Trade Union €8.63 VHI €12.75

EMPLOYEE PROFILE

Employee No. 5	
Name:	Teresa Kelly
Address:	18 Goldenbridge Rd, Inchicore, Dublin 8
PPS No.	3492426L
Cost Code:	Accounts
Pay method:	Cheque
Gross salary (weekly):	€550.00
Tax status:	Normal
Tax credit:	€47.85
Cut-off point:	€540.00
PRSI Class:	A
Insurable weeks:	50
Start date with the company:	21-06-1998
Gross earnings (less pension) YTD:	€27,500.00
Tax paid YTD:	€3,531.00
Net earnings YTD:	€21,004.00
PRSI paid YTD:	EE = €1,396.00
PRSI paid YTD:	ER = €3,300.00
Pension paid YTD:	EE = Nil

Timesheet entries

	Payment	Deductions
Week 51	Commission €50.00 Bonus €32.00 Expenses €45.50	Trade Union €8.63 VHI €22.75

Additional information:
Teresa left the company in December. Enter the following details:
Finish date: 21 December 200_
Finish period: 51

Revision Assignments

PROJECT BRIEF

BACKGROUND

Company Name: Phoenix Ltd
Address: 12 Grosvenor Rd, Rathmines, Dublin 6
Registration No. 5926432M
Company Directors: Matthew and Helen O'Sullivan

INSTRUCTIONS TO CANDIDATES

You work in the HR Department and your job is to maintain the company's payroll. Your tasks are as follows:

1. PAYROLL PROCESSING

(i) Process the payroll for four of the employees from the data supplied on pages 114 to 116.

2. TAX RETURN FORMS

(i) Complete the P45 and P60 for the appropriate employees.
(ii) Complete the P30 for the month ended 31 December, 200_.
(iii) Complete the P35L and P35 for the year ended 31 December, 200_.
Note: The company submitted the following amounts to the Collector General during the year: €17,485 PAYE and €10,300 PRSI.

3. TAXATION

Complete the following tasks on page 117:

(i) Tax treatment of married couples under single and joint assessment
(ii) Calculation of change in annual take-home salary due to effect of new budget.

EMPLOYEE PROFILE

Employee No. 1	
Name:	Brendan Ryan
Address:	18 Merrion Rd, Ballsbridge, Dublin 4
PPS No:	3565771J
Start date with the company:	July 1996
Basic wage (weekly):	€487.50
Basic hours:	39
Tax type:	Normal
Tax credit:	€45.92
Cut-off point:	€542.50
Earnings YTD:	€20,806.50
Tax paid YTD:	€2,317.62
PRSI paid YTD (EE):	€1,063.48
PRSI paid YTD (TOT):	€3,369.52
PRSI Class:	A
Pension Contribution:	3%
Weekly Deductions:	Union €7.50 and VHI €23.50

Task

1. Process Brendan's payroll for each week from 8 November, 200_.
2. During the week beginning 15 November Brendan worked overtime as follows: Monday – 4 hours, Wednesday – 5 hours and Saturday – 4 hours.
   Refer to the overtime rates on page 6 of your textbook.
3. He took two weeks' holidays from the week beginning 29 November for which he was paid in advance.
4. He left the company on 20 December for a new job.
5. Prepare a P45 for Brendan on the day he leaves work.

Revision Assignments

EMPLOYEE PROFILE

Employee No. 2	
Name:	Robert Moore
Address:	26 Waterloo Rd, Ballsbridge, Dublin 4
PPS No:	1285988J
Start date with the company:	10 October this year
Basic salary (weekly):	€320.00
Tax type:	Emergency
Earnings YTD:	Nil
Tax paid YTD:	Nil
PRSI paid YTD (EE):	Nil
PRSI paid YTD (TOT):	Nil
PRSI Class:	A
Pension Contribution:	None

Task

1. Process Robert's payroll from 16 October to the end of the tax year.
2. Robert was transferred to the cumulative tax system on 18 December, 200_ after his cumulative TDC and tax credit certificate were issued. On the cumulative system his weekly tax credit is €45.80 and his weekly cut-off point is €540.00.

EMPLOYEE PROFILE

Employee No. 3	
Name:	Fiona Shaw
Address:	6 The Maples, Greenlea Dr., Terenure, Dublin 6
PPS No:	5282041K
Start date with the company:	28 November this year
Basic salary (weekly):	€450.00
Tax type:	Week 1/Month 1
Tax credit:	Calculate from the data below
Cut-off point:	€542.50
Earnings YTD (previous employer):	€18,900.00
Tax paid YTD (previous employer):	€1,460.70
PRSI paid YTD (EE):	€905.40
PRSI paid YTD (TOT):	€2,937.15
PRSI Class:	A
Pension Contribution:	None

Note

Fiona is entitled to the following tax credits

(i) Personal (widowed for two years)

(ii) PAYE

(iii) Eight-year-old daughter with a physical disability.

Task

1. Process Fiona's payroll for each week from 6 December, 200_.
2. Prepare her P60, which she receives at the end of the tax year.

EMPLOYEE PROFILE

Employee No. 4	
Name:	David Cairns
Address:	23 Terenure Rd West, Dublin 6
PPS No:	45897254L
Start date with the company:	August 1992
Basic salary (monthly):	€3,500.00
Pension contribution:	5 %
Tax type:	Normal
Tax credit:	202.65
Cut-off point:	€2,350.50
Earnings YTD:	€28,500.00
Tax paid YTD:	€4,772.40
PRSI paid YTD (EE):	€1,501.20
PRSI paid YTD (TOT):	€4,565.00
PRSI Class:	A

Task

Process David's payroll for the months of November and December, 200_.

TAXATION

Tax Treatment of Married Couples

Tom and Helen are a married couple with salaries of €40,000 and €22,500 respectively. They are entitled to the basic tax credits and cut-off point. They have a three-year-old son with special needs who is maintained in the proportion 2:1 as to Helen and Tom. Helen's aged mother lives with the family also.

You are required to:

(i) calculate the income tax payable by this couple using both single and joint assessment methods;
(ii) indicate, by how much, which assessment method is most tax efficient.

Impact of the Budget on Take-Home Pay

John is single, earning €38,500. He is entitled to the basic tax credits and cut-off point.

You are required to:

(i) calculate John's take-home pay for the current tax year and his take-home pay next year based on the projected changes announced in the budget;
(ii) indicate by how much John will be better or worse off next year compared to the current tax year.

Quiz Answers

The following are the correct answers to the quiz on pages 103–4, showing the relevant chapter and page numbers.

1. False Ch 1 page 2
2. False Ch 3 page 33
3. False Ch 5 page 68
4. False Ch 2 page 9
5. True Ch 3 page 23
6. False Ch 2 page 17
7. True Ch 2 page 8
8. True Ch 2 page 18
9. False Ch 1 page 3
10. False Ch 2 page 14
11. True Ch 2 page 14
12. False Ch 3 page 24
13. True Ch 3 page 25
14. True Ch 3 page 25
15. False Ch 3 page 23
16. True Ch 3 page 33
17. False Ch 4 page 52
18. True Ch 5 page 63
19. False Ch 5 page 68
20. False Ch 6 pages 79, 80

Appendix A

Income Tax Calendar

This appendix contains the following sections:
- income tax weeks
- income tax months.

INCOME TAX WEEKS

Week Number	Period covered (both dates inclusive)
1	January 1 – January 7
2	8 – 14
3	15 – 21
4	22 – 28
5	January 29 – February 4
6	5 – 11
7	12 – 18
8	19 – 25
9	February 26 – March 4 (Normal years)
10	5 – 11
11	12 – 18
12	19 – 25
13	March 26 – April 1
14	2 – 8
15	9 – 15
16	16 – 22
17	23 – 29
18	April 30 – May 6
19	7 – 13
20	14 – 20
21	21 – 27
22	May 28 – June 3
23	4 – 10
24	11 – 17
25	18 – 24
26	June 25 – 1 July

27	2 – 8
28	9 – 15
29	16 – 22
30	23 – 29
31	July 30 – Aug 5
32	6 – 12
33	13 – 19
34	20 – 26
35	August 27 – September 2
36	3 – 9
37	10 – 16
38	17 – 23
39	24 – 30
40	October 1 – 7
41	8 – 14
42	15 – 21
43	22 – 28
44	October 29 – November 4
45	5 – 11
46	12 – 18
47	19 – 25
48	26 – December 2
49	3 – 9
50	10 – 16
51	17 – 23
52	24 – 30
53	December 31 (where it is a pay day)
53	December 30 and 31 (leap year pay days)

INCOME TAX MONTHS

Month Number	Period covered (both dates inclusive)
1	January 1 – January 31
2	February 1 – February 28 (Normal years)
3	March 1 – March 31
4	April 1 – April 30
5	May 1 – May 31
6	June 1 – June 30
7	July 1 – July 31
8	August 1 – August 31
9	September 1 – September 30
10	October 1 – October 31
11	November 1 – November 30
12	December 1 – December 31

Appendix B

PRSI Rates of Contribution for a Sample Tax Year

This appendix contains the following sections:
- Class A PRSI rates
- Class B PRSI rates
- Class D PRSI rates.

CLASS A PRSI RATES

TABLE B.1 CLASS A PRSI RATES

Weekly Earnings Band	Amount of Weekly Earnings		First €42,160	Balance Over €42,160
Class A0 €38.00 – €287.00	All All	Employer Employee	8.50 % 0.00 %	8.50 % 0.00 %
Class AX €287.01 – €356.00	All First €127 Balance	Employer Employee Employee	8.50 % 0.00 % 4.00 %	8.50 % 0.00 % 0.00 %
Class A1 In excess €356.00	All First €127 Balance	Employer Employee Employee	10.75 % 2.00 % 6.00 %	10.75 % 2.00 % 2.00 %

Notes: 1. The earnings threshold applies to the *employee* only.
2. If monthly paid, the PRSI-free amount is €551.00

People in class A

The following people are in class A: people in industrial, commercial, and service-type employment who are employed under a contract of service with reckonable earnings of €38.09 or more per week from all employments. Public Servants recruited *from* 6 April 1995 are also in class A.

CLASS B PRSI RATES

TABLE B.2 CLASS B PRSI RATES

Weekly Earnings Band	Amount of Weekly Earnings		First €42,160	Balance Over €42,160
Class B0 Up to €287.00	All All	Employer Employee	2.01% 0.00 %	2.01 % 0.00 %
Class BX €287.01 — €356.00	All First €26 Balance	Employer Employee Employee	2.01 % 0.00 % 0.90 %	2.01 % 0.00 % 0.00 %
Class B1 In excess €356.00	All First €26 Balance	Employer Employee Employee	2.01 % 2.00 % 2.90 %	2.01 % 2.00% 2.00%

Note: The earnings threshold applies to the *employee* only.

People in class B

The following people are in class B: permanent and pensionable civil servants recruited *before* 6 April 1995; registered doctors and dentists employed in the civil service and Gardai.

CLASS D PRSI RATES

TABLE B.3 CLASS D PRSI RATES

Weekly Earnings Band	Amount of Weekly Earnings		First €42,160	Balance Over €42,160
Class D0 Up to €287.00	All All	Employer Employee	2.35 % 0.00 %	2.35 % 0.00 %
Class DX €287.01 – €356.00	All First €26 Balance	Employer Employee Employee	2.35 % 0.00 % 0.90 %	2.35 % 0.00 % 0.00 %
Class D1 In excess €356.00	All First €26 Balance	Employer Employee Employee	2.35 % 2.00 % 2.90 %	2.35 % 2.00% 2.00%

Note: The earnings threshold applies to the *employee* only.

People in class D

The following people are in class D: permanent and pensionable employees in the public service, other than those mentioned in Class B, recruited *before* 6 April 1995.

Appendix C

PRSI Rates of Contribution for the Current Tax Year

This appendix contains the following sections:
- Class A PRSI rates
- Class B PRSI rates
- Class D PRSI rates.

CLASS A PRSI RATES

TABLE C.1 CLASS A PRSI RATES

Weekly Earnings Band	Amount of Weekly Earnings		Up to € %	In Excess of € %
Class A0 € — €	All All	Employer Employee		
Class AX € — €	All First € Balance	Employer Employee Employee		
Class A1 In excess €	All First € Balance	Employer Employee Employee		

Note: The earnings threshold applies to the *employee* only.
If paid monthly, the PRSI-free amount is €

CLASS B PRSI RATES

TABLE C.2 CLASS B PRSI RATES

Weekly Earnings Band	Amount of Weekly Earnings		Up to € %	In Excess of € %
Class B0 Up to €	All All	Employer Employee		
Class BX € – €	All First € Balance	Employer Employee Employee		
Class B1 In excess €	All First € Balance	Employer Employee Employee		

Note: The earnings threshold applies to the *employee* only.

CLASS D PRSI RATES

TABLE C.3 CLASS D PRSI RATES

Weekly Earnings Band	Amount of Weekly Earnings		Up to € %	In Excess of € %
Class D0 Up to €	All All	Employer Employee		
Class DX € – €	All First € Balance	Employer Employee Employee		
Class D1 In excess €	All First € Balance	Employer Employee Employee		

Note: The earnings threshold applies to the *employee* only.
If paid monthly, the PRSI-free amount is €   .

Appendix D

Tax Rates, Bands and Credits for the Current Tax Year

You can find the relevant up-to-date information on tax and PRSI by contacting the following information offices and by accessing the web addresses mentioned.

- Your local tax office.
- Information offices of the Revenue Commissioners at one of the following locations:
  — Cathedral St, Dublin 1
  — Level 2, The Square, Tallaght, Dublin 24
  — 85/93 Lower Mount St, Dublin 2.
- Revenue Forms and Leaflets service, telephone Lo-call 1890 - 30 67 06.
- The Revenue website is very good and can be accessed on www.revenue.ie
- An up-to-date PAYE/PRSI information pack with ready reckoner may be obtained from the Department of Social and Family Affairs, Gandon House, Amiens St, Dublin 1, telephone (01) 7043274.
- The Welfare website can be accessed on www.welfare.ie

TAX RATES

Table D.1 shows information on tax rates. You can insert the figures for the current year in the spaces provided.

TABLE D.1 CURRENT TAX RATES

Description	Current Rate
Standard Rate	%
Higher Rate	%

TAX BAND

This is a fixed amount of taxable income that is taxed at the standard rate of tax. Any taxable pay exceeding the band amount is taxed at the higher rate. You can insert the figures for the current year in the spaces provided in Table D.2.

TABLE D.2 TAX BANDS FOR THE CURRENT TAX YEAR

Personal Status	Band of Taxable Income
Single / widowed without dependent child(ren)	€ @ % Balance @ %
Single / widowed with dependent child(ren)	€ @ % Balance @ %
Married couple (one spouse with income)	€ @ % Balance @ %
Married couple (both spouses with income)	€ @ % (with an increase of € max) Balance @ %

THE STANDARD RATE CUT-OFF POINT

This is an amount which is equivalent to the tax band. However, the cut-off point can be adjusted depending on a taxpayer's personal circumstances. Items such as benefits-in-kind and employment expenses cause variations in the cut-off point from one taxpayer to another.

TAX CREDITS

Employees can claim a number of credits which help reduce their tax bill. Table D.3 lists the main tax credits for the tax year. You can insert the figures for the current year in the spaces provided.

TABLE D.3 TAX CREDITS FOR THE CURRENT YEAR

Personal Status	Credits
Single Person	€
Married Person	€
Widowed Person	
Without dependent child(ren)	€
With dependent child(ren)	€
One-Parent Family	
Widowed Person	€
Other Person	€
Widowed Parent	
Bereaved in Year 1	€
Year 2	€
Year 3	€
Year 4	€
Year 5	€
PAYE (individual)	€
Incapacitated Child (max)	€
Dependent Relative (max)	€
Home Carer (max)	€
Trade Union Subscription (max)	€
	€

EMERGENCY TAX DATA

TABLE D.4 TAX CREDITS AND TAX RATES FOR AN EMPLOYEE PAID ON A WEEKLY BASIS IN THE CURRENT TAX YEAR

Week of Employment	Tax Credit Amount	Tax Rate
First	€	Lower Rate
Second	€	Lower Rate
Third	€	Lower Rate
Fourth	€	Lower Rate
Each of Next Four	Nil	Lower Rate
Each Week Thereafter	Nil	Higher Rate

TABLE D.5 TAX CREDITS AND TAX RATES FOR AN EMPLOYEE PAID ON A MONTHLY BASIS IN THE CURRENT TAX YEAR

Month of Employment	Tax Credit Amount	Tax Rate
First	€	Lower Rate
Second	Nil	Lower Rate
Each Month Thereafter	Nil	Higher Rate

Appendix E

Tax and PRSI Data for a Selection of Years

Insert the relevant data for the appropriate years.

	2000/01	2001	2002	2003	2004	2005	2006	2007
TAX RATES								
Standard tax rate	22%	20%	20%	20%	20%			
Higher tax rate	44%	42%	42%	42%	42%			
TAX BANDS	€	€	€	€	€	€	€	€
Single tax band	21,586	25,395	28,000	28,000	28,000			
Married tax band*	43,172	50,790	56,000	56,000	56,000			
TAX CREDITS								
Single personal credit	1,313	1,397	1,520	1,520	1,520			
Married personal credit	2,626	2,794	3,040	3,040	3,040			
PAYE credit	279	508	660	800	1,040			
Dependent relative (max)	62	56	60	60	60			
Incapacitated child (max)	447	406	500	500	500			
PRSI RATES								
PRSI class A1 ceiling	€33,648	€35,870	€35,870	€40,420	€42,160			
First €6,604	2.00%	2.00%	2.00%	2.00%	2.00%			
Balance	6.50%	6.00%	6.00%	6.00%	6.00%			

* **Note:** Assume both spouses working and their earnings exceed band thresholds.

Appendix F

List of PAYE Forms That Employers Use

This appendix lists the PAYE forms that employers use.

Supplies of the following forms are issued to all employers who are registered for PAYE:

- P8/P15   Instruction form on completion of tax deduction card, emergency card and temporary tax deduction form.
- P13/P14   Emergency card/temporary tax deduction form.
- P45   Four-part cessation certificate.
- P45 (supplement) Particulars of payments made to employee after leaving.
- P46   Employer's notification to Inspector of Taxes about commencement of new employee.
- P50   Employee's application to Inspector of Taxes for refund during unemployment.
- P61   Tax tables, ready-reckoners.

If you want more of these forms, use form P34 to request them.

The Inspector of Taxes also issues the following forms:

- P2C   Certificate of tax credits and cut-off point.
- P9/P11   Tax deduction card.
- P11D   Return of benefits, non-cash emoluments, etc. to or for directors and certain employees.
- Reg. 2   To be completed by an employer when applying for registration.

The Collector-General issues the following forms:

- P9L/P11L   End-of-year forms lodged by employers using a computer system in cases where emergency or temporary tax was used at the end of the tax year, or where an employee's PPS number is not known.
- P30 Bank giro/payslip Employer's remittance form (income tax and PRSI contributions).
- P35   Employer's remittance declaration of liability for tax and PRSI contributions.

List of PAYE Forms That Employers Use

- P35L and P35L/T   Employer's annual return of pay, tax, PRSI data, etc. in respect of each employee.
- P60   Employer's certificate of pay, tax deducted and PRSI contributions for the year.

Employers of casual employees use the following forms:

- P13D   Emergency tax deduction card
- P28   Daily tax deduction card
- P28-1   Supplementary daily tax deduction card
- P29   Employer's return to Collector-General
- P29L   List of casual employees.

Appendix G

Copies of Various Tax Forms

You can use the following forms to complete assignments. This appendix contains the following forms:

- Figure G.1 Official Cumulative Tax Deduction Card
- Figure G.2 Employee Tax Deduction Card
- Figure G.3 Emergency/Temporary Tax Deduction Card
- Figure G.4 Form P30 – Employer's Remittance Form
- Figure G.5 Form P45 – Cessation Certificate
- Figure G.6 Form P60 – Certificate of Pay, Tax, and PRSI
- Figure G.7 Form P35L – List of Employees with RSI Numbers
- Figure G.8 Form P35 – Declaration of Tax and PRSI for All Employees

Copies of Various Tax Forms

FIGURE G.1 OFFICIAL CUMULATIVE TAX DEDUCTION CARD

Revenue

TAX DEDUCTION CARD
TDCGA.FRM

Incorporating Certificate of Tax Credits and Standard Rate Cut-off Point

The Tax Credits and Standard Rate Cut-off Point set out on this card refer to
These instructions cancel any previously issued card for the year   to
If you have any problems with the operation of this card please refer to the Notice to Employers issued by the Tax Office. You can obtain a copy by phoning your local Tax Office or in Dublin by phoning Revenue Forms and Leaflets Service at :
Lo-Call No. 1890 306 706.

EMPLOYER'S Name & Address

Employer's Number   Date of Issue

This Tax Deduction Card is effective from

and should be implemented accordingly

EMPLOYEE DETAILS

PPS Number   Works Number (N6)

Name   Year
                                    TO

Total Tax Credit   Total Cut-Off Point

Standard Tax Rate: ____ %
Higher Tax Rate: ____ %

Columns headed "For Employer's Use" may be used by YOU for making whatever entries YOU require e.g. net pay, employer's PRSI etc.

The PPS number must be quoted on all official forms and in any correspondence referring to this employee.

Issued by:

A	B		C	D	E		F
Date of Payment	See PAYE Calendar		PRSI Employee's Share	PRSI Total Contribution	Social Ins weekly record Insurable Employment	PRSI Class	For Employer use Net pay, Employers PRSI etc
	Month	Week	€ c	€ c			€ c
		1					
1 Jan. to 31 Jan.		2					
		3					
		4					
	1	5					
1 Feb. to 28 Feb.		6					
		7					
		8					
	2	9					
1 Mar. to 31 Mar.		10					
		11					
		12					
	3	13					
1 Apr. to 30 Apr.		14					
		15					
		16					
		17					
	4	18					
1 May to 31 May		19					
		20					
		21					
	5	22					
1 June to 30 June		23					
		24					
		25					
	6	26					
1 July to 31 July		27					
		28					
		29					
		30					
	7	31					
1 Aug. to 31 Aug.		32					
		33					
		34					
	8	35					
1 Sept. to 30 Sept.		36					
		37					
		38					
	9	39					
1 Oct. to 31 Oct.		40					
		41					
		42					
		43					
	10	44					
1 Nov. to 30 Nov.		45					
		46					
		47					
	11	48					
1 Dec. to 31 Dec.		49					
		50					
		51					
		52					
	12	53					
		K3					
		K4		↑ F2	Total Weeks		

P9/P11

If the person to whom this card refers is not now in your employment or leaves your employment before 31st December next please return this card to the address shown above. If employee leaves your employment during the year to which this card refers, you should complete form P45 Cessation Certificate

C2 ____   Initial Class

Social Insurance Class

IF Class changed during this employment complete these boxes
Date of Change

B4 ____   C3 ____   Other Class   F3 ____   Weeks at Other Class

N.B If more than two classes please furnish details on Form PRC 1

Payroll—Manual and Computerised

TDCGE.FRM

| Employee's Name | | PPS Number | Works No. | Total Tax Credit | Total Cut-Off | Date of Issue |

Week No.	G Gross Pay (less Superannuation) this Period	H Cumulative Gross Pay to Date	I Cumulative Standard Rate Cut-Off point	J Cumulative Tax due at Standard Rate	K Cumulative Tax due at Higher Rate	L Cumulative Gross tax	M Cumulative Tax Credit	N Cumulative Tax (cannot be less than 0)	O Tax Deducted this Period	P Tax Refunded this Period
	€ c	€ c	€ c	€ c	€ c	€ c	€ c	€ c	€ c	€ c
1										
2										
3										
... through 53										

J6 ← Pay   Previous Employment DEDUCT   Tax →
            This Employment Net Tax deducted or Net Tax refunded   J7
            H9

F4 / F5   Day Month Year
If employment ceased during the tax year enter date of cessation at F5
If employment began (a) in Week 1 or later or (b) before Week 1 but first pay day was in Week 1 or later, enter date of commencement at F4

Copies of Various Tax Forms 135

FIGURE G.2 OWN SYSTEM TAX DEDUCTION CARD

FIGURE G.3 EMERGENCY/TEMPORARY TAX DEDUCTION CARD

Temporary/Emergency Tax Deduction Card
For the Tax Year Ended 31 December 200

EMPLOYER'S Name & Address

Employer's Number
EMPLOYEE DETAILS

PPS Number   Works Number (N6)

Name   Period

Standard Tax Rate: 20%   Higher Tax Rate: 42%

This Tax Deduction Card (TDC) can be used as an Emergency TDC or a Temporary TDC

Used as Emergency Card ☐   Used as a Temporary Card ☐

Use this as an Emergency TDC when:

- You have **not** received either a certificate of Tax Credits and Standard Rate Cut-Off Point or a form P45 for the current year, **or**
- You receive a P45 from an employee which indicates that emergency tax applied in the previous employment, **or**
- The employee has given the employer a completed P45 without a PPS number and not indicating that the emergency basis applies.

Tax is calculated on the gross pay (after deduction of pension contributions and permanent health contributions where relevant). Different rules apply depending on whether or not the employee provides an employer with his/her PPS number.

The tables below outline the tax credits and cut-off points applicable.

The standard rate of tax is 20%. The higher rate of tax is 42%

Employee does not provide a PPS Number

Week or Month	Cut-Off Point	Tax Credit
All	0.00	0.00

Employee does provide a PPS Number

Weekly Paid	Cut-Off Point	Tax Credit
Week 1 to 4		
Week 5 to 8		
Week 9 onwards		

Monthly Paid	Cut-Off Point	Tax Credit
Month 1		
Month 2		
Month 3 onwards		

Where for example an employee starts employment without a PPS Number, provides it in say week 3, but still has not provided a P45 or Tax Credit Certificate, tax should be applied at Week 3 per the schedule listed above and continued into Week 4 and 5 etc., as appropriate, until such time as a P45 or Tax Credit Certificate is provided.

Use this as a Temporary TDC when:

- You have received a P45 from an employee which indicates the Tax Credits and Standard Rate Cut-Off Point to be used.

Detailed notes on relevant entries are included overleaf.

P13/P14

A Date of Payment	B See PAYE Calendar (Month / Week)	C PRSI Employee's Share	D PRSI Total contribution	E Social Ins weekly record
1 Jan. to 31 Jan	1			
	2			
	3			
	4			
1	5			
1 Feb. to 28 Feb.	6			
	7			
	8			
2	9			
1 Mar. to 31 Mar.	10			
	11			
	12			
3	13			
1 Apr. to 30 Apr.	14			
	15			
	16			
	17			
4	18			
1 May to 31 May	19			
	20			
	21			
5	22			
1 June to 30 June	23			
	24			
	25			
6	26			
1 July to 31 July	27			
	28			
	29			
	30			
7	31			
1 Aug. to 31 Aug.	32			
	33			
	34			
8	35			
1 Sept. to 30 Sept.	36			
	37			
	38			
9	39			
1 Oct. to 31 Oct.	40			
	41			
	42			
	43			
10	44			
1 Nov. to 30 Nov.	45			
	46			
	47			
11	48			
1 Dec. to 31 Dec.	49			
	50			
	51			
	52			
12	53			
		K3		Total Weeks
		K4	F2	

C2 ☐   **Social Insurance Class**
IF Class changed during this employment complete these boxes

Initial Class	Date of Change	Other Class	Weeks at Other Class
	B4	C3	F3

N.B. If more than two classes please furnish details on Form PRC 1

Week No.	F Gross Pay (Less Superannuation) This Period		G Standard Rate Cut-Off Point This Period		H Tax Due at Standard Rate This Period		I Tax Due at Higher Rate This Period		J Gross Tax This Period		K Tax Credit This Period		L Tax Due this Period		M For Employer Use		Description of Entry for each Column
	€	c	€	c	€	c	€	c	€	c	€	c	€	c	€	c	
1																	
2																	**Column C, D, E**
3																	
4																	PRSI Details
5																	
6																	**Column F**
7																	Gross pay: (Including overtime, bonus, commissions etc.) after deduction of any Superannuation and contributions to a Revenue Approved permanent health benefit scheme payable and allowable for income tax purposes.
...																	
53																	

J6 ← Pay   Tax → J7

Day Month Year
F4 [ ][ ][ ]
F5 [ ][ ][ ]

If employment ceased during the tax year enter date of cessation at F5

If employment began
(a) in Week 1 or later, or
(b) before Week 1 but first pay day was in Week 1 or later, enter date of commencement at F4

Column G
Temporary TDC: Standard rate cut-off point as shown on Form P45.
Emergency TDC: See notes overleaf

Column H
Tax due at standard rate of tax this period

Column I
Tax due at higher rate of tax this period

Column J
Gross tax this period

Column K
Temporary TDC: Tax credits as shown on Form P45.
Emergency TDC: See notes overleaf

Column L
Tax due for this period

Column M
Freeflow e.g., net pay, employer's PRSI etc.

FIGURE G.4 FORM P30 – EMPLOYER'S REMITTANCE FORM

In all Correspondence Please quote
Registration No: 1234567A
Notice No.: 1234567-00001A

Office of the Revenue Commissioners
Collector-Generals Division
Sarsfield House
Francis Street
Limerick

MR BARNEY RUBBLE
C/O FLINTSTONES & CO
COBBLESTONE PLACE
BEDROCK
CO DUBLIN

Enquiries: 1890203070

INCOME TAX (PAYE), SOCIAL INSURANCE, CONTRIBUTIONS AND LEVIES (PRSI)

Please see notes overleaf regarding completion and method of payment.

Period:
Payment due not later than:

These amounts are your own record of PAYE/PRSI remitted. These details must also be entered in the boxes on the payslip below.

	€
PAYE	
PRSI	
TOTAL	

€ (Currency)

Please do not photocopy this form or payslip or use it for any other period or customer.
Always return the payslip even for nil returns.

BANK GIRO CREDIT TRANSFER **Payslip** **P30** **Revenue**

Name: MR BARNEY RUBBLE
Period:
I declare that the amount shown below is the amount I am liable to remit to the Collector-General for the above period.

Signed:_____ Date:_____

Registration No: 1234567A
Notice No: 1234567-00001A
Date Rec'd

	€	
PAYE		00
PRSI		00
TOTAL		00

Whole Euros only. Please do not enter cents.

Receiving Cashier's Brand & Initials.

CHEQUES	
TOTAL €	

Please do not fold this payslip or write or mark below this line.

P30 (EUR)

90 7104 9328844 71

FIGURE G.5 FORM P45 – CESSATION CERTIFICATE

FORM P45

CERTIFICATE NO. **U683377**

INCOME TAX - PAY AS YOU EARN - CESSATION CERTIFICATE
Particulars of Employee Leaving

PLEASE COMPLETE FORM IN BLOCK CAPITALS

Surname
First Name(s)
Unit Number
PPS Number
Date of Leaving
Address
Employer Registered Number
Date of Birth
Payroll/Works No.
Deceased (Tick ✔ if applicable)
Commencement

○ Weekly   ○ Monthly (Please tick ✔ if you are paid weekly or Monthly)

Weekly/Monthly Tax Credit
Week/Month Number
Weekly/Monthly Standard Rate Cut-Off Point
Tick ✔ if emergency tax operated

(a) **TOTAL PAY & TAX** deducted from 1 January last to date of leaving

Total Pay   Total Tax Deducted

(b) If Employment commenced since 1 January last enter Pay and Tax deducted for this period of employment only

Pay   Tax Deducted

(c) Amount of Taxable **LUMP SUM PAYMENT** on termination included in either pay figure above - if applicable

(a) Total amount of Taxable Disability Benefit included in Total Pay above
(b) Amount by which Tax Credits were reduced
    Amount by which Standard Rate Cut-Off Point was reduced
(c) Indicate that Week 1/Month 1 basis was applied   (Tick ✔ if applicable)

Please complete **A, B or C** across where an employee was in receipt of taxable Disability Benefit since 1st January last while employed by you

PRSI - THIS EMPLOYMENT ONLY

Total PRSI   Total number of weeks of Insurable Employment
Employee's Share   Total number of weeks at Class A or Subclass "A" in this period
                     PRSI Classes other than Class A or Subclass "A" in this period

I certify that the particulars entered above are correct.

Employer   Trade name if different
Address   Date   Phone No.
                      Fax No.

Revenue On-Line Service   Save Time File P45's on-line using the Revenue On-Line Service.   www.revenue.ie

INSTRUCTIONS TO EMPLOYER
(a) Complete this form when an employee leaves your employment. Take care that all entries are in BLOCK capitals.
(b) Copy PPS Number, Tax Credits, and Standard Rate Cut-Off Point from the latest Certificate of Tax Credits and Standard Rate Cut-Off Point.
(c) If the employee commenced with you after 1st January last include pay and tax notified to you in respect of previous employment. Please insert date of commencement if after the start of this tax year.
(d) Detach Part 1 and send it to your Tax Office immediately. Hand Parts 2, 3 and 4 (unseparated) to the employee when he/she leaves.
(e) If employee has died please send ALL FOUR PARTS of this form (unseparated) to your Tax Office immediately.
(f) A guide to PAYE / PRSI for small employers (IT 50) is available from our Forms & Leaflets Service 1890 306 706 or the Revenue Website.

PART 1

FIGURE G.6 FORM P60 – CERTIFICATE OF PAY, TAX, AND PRSI

P60 PAYE/PRSI
CERTIFICATE OF PAY, TAX AND PAY-RELATED SOCIAL INSURANCE FOR 200_
TO BE GIVEN TO EACH EMPLOYEE WHO WAS IN YOUR EMPLOYMENT ON 31 DECEMBER 200_ WHETHER OR NOT TAX WAS DEDUCTED

NAME ....

ADDRESS ....

Personal Public Service No. (PPS No.)

If at 31 December 200_
Temporary basis applied enter "1"
Emergency basis applied enter "2"

Week 1/Month 1 basis applied enter "W"

| Tax Credit € | Standard Rate Cut Off Point € | Works Number | Date of Commencement | Enter only if date is after 1 Jan 200_ |

Employers Unit Code

If the employee was not in any other employment during the period 1 Jan 200_ to 31 December 200_, the employer need not complete lines 1 and 2 at A and B below. Lines A3 and B3 must always be completed. If an entry is made at line A1 it should equal the sum of the amounts at lines A2 and A3.

A
PAY — € c
1. Total pay in year to 31 December 200_ (including pay in respect of previous employment(s), if any) ....
2. Pay in year in respect of previous employment(s), if any, in the year to 31 December 200_ taken into account arriving at the tax deductions made by me/us ....
3. Pay in respect of THIS employment (i.e. gross pay less superannuation contributions allowable for income tax purposes) **J6**

B
TAX — € c
1. Total net tax deducted in year ended 31 December 200_ (including tax deducted by previous employer(s), if any) ....
2. Tax in respect of previous employment(s), if any, in the year to 31 December 200_ ....
3. Net tax deducted in respect of THIS employment **J7**
   OR
   Net tax repaid in respect of THIS employment **H9**

C
PRSI IN THIS EMPLOYMENT — € c
1. Employee's share of pay-related social insurance contribution **K3**
2. Total (i.e. employee's and employer's shares) of pay-related social insurance contribution **K4**
3. Total number of weeks of insurable employment inclusive of the number of weeks, if any, at line 6 below **F2**
4. Social insurance contribution class at 1 Jan 200_ or at such later date as employment commenced **C2**
5. Second social insurance contribution class/subclass if class changed during this employment **C3**
6. Number of weeks of insurable employment at the class entered at line 5 .... **F3**

I/We certify that the particulars given above include the total amount of pay (including overtime, bonus, commission, etc.) paid to you by me/us in the year ended 31 December 200_ the total tax deducted by me/us less any refunds and the total pay-related social insurance contribution in respect of this employment.

P1 Employer's Registered Number

Employer .... Date ....

TO THE EMPLOYEE: **THIS IS A VALUABLE DOCUMENT.**

You should retain it carefully as evidence of tax deducted from your income:-

You may also require this document for production to the Collector General if you are claiming repayment of:

(a) PRSI contributions on pay in excess of the pay ceiling for contribution purposes or
(b) the Health Contribution where income was below the relevant threshold for the year.

Form P60 (Rev).

FIGURE G.7 FORM P35L – LIST OF EMPLOYEES WITH RSI NUMBERS

FIGURE G.8 FORM P35 – DECLARATION OF TAX AND PRSI FOR ALL EMPLOYEES

List of Abbreviations

BIK	Benefit-in-Kind
CPU	Central Processing Unit
EE	Employee
EFT	Electronic Funds Transfer
EMT	Electronic Money Transfer
ER	Employer
PAYE	Pay As You Earn
PPS	Personal Public Service (number)
PRSA	Personal Retirement Savings Account
PRSI	Pay Related Social Insurance
RDI	ROS Debit Instruction
ROS	Revenue On-line Service
TDC	Tax Deduction Card
TRS	Tax Relief at Source
YTD	Year To Date